D1054440

BRINGING HIDDEN THINGS TO LIGHT

BRINGING HIDDEN THINGS TO LIGHT

THE REVIVAL OF METHODISM IN RUSSIA

LYDIA P. ISTOMINA

translated by
Lucy Smolenskaya

ABINGDON PRESS
Nashville

BRINGING HIDDEN THINGS TO LIGHT
The Revival of Methodism in Russia

Copyright © 1996 by Abingdon Press

All rights reserved.
No part of this work may be reproduced or transmitted in any form or by any means, electronic or mechanical, including photocopying and recording, or by any information storage or retrieval system, except as may be expressly permitted by the 1976 Copyright Act or in writing from the publisher. Requests for permission should be addressed to Abingdon Press, P.O. Box 801, 201 Eighth Avenue South, Nashville, TN 37202-0871.

This book is printed on recycled, acid-free paper.

Library of Congress Cataloging-in-Publication Data

Istomina, Lydia P., 1956–
    Bringing hidden things to light: the revival of Methodism in Russia/Lydia P. Istomina: translated by Lucy Smolenskaya.
      p. cm.
    ISBN 0-687-10923-X (pbk.: alk. paper)
    1. Istomina, Lydia P., 1956– . 2. United Methodist Church (U.S.)—Russia (Federation)—Ekaterinburg—Clergy—Biography.
3. United Methodist Church (U.S.)—Russia (Federation)—History.
4. Ekaterinburg (Russia)—Church history—20th century.
5. Methodist Church—Russia (Federation)—History—20th century.
6. Russia (Federation)—Church history—20th century. I. Title.
BX8495.I77A3   1996
287'.647—dc20   96-383
                                                  CIP

Scripture quotations are from the New Revised Standard Version Bible, copyright © 1989, by the Division of Christian Education of the National Council of the Churches of Christ in the USA.

96 97 98 99 00 01 02 03 04 05—10 9 8 7 6 5 4 3 2 1

MANUFACTURED IN THE UNITED STATES OF AMERICA

*L*ooking at old photos, even while listening to explanations, you still must find it impossible to grasp the full depth and meaning of past events caught by the camera if you didn't take part in them. Old photos are always an enigma, a mystery. These people from the past, long dead, once young, loving or loved, smiling, grieving—where are they? Often we don't even remember their names.

Today as I spread on my table the photos from the early 1900s, snapshots of the first Methodists in Russia, people who were humiliated, oppressed, tormented, I can see their eyes, feel their presence, hear their voices. They tell me that I must write about the events that are happening now to us, their followers. I write this book lest the names of the present-day Methodists living in Russia should be forgotten. I write in order that life in the church should continue in our children, grandchildren, and all our descendants, no matter what happens in our capricious history. I write so our photos should not be silent pictures. And I dedicate this book to my closest and dearest friends—my children: Julia and Paul.

ACKNOWLEDGMENTS

I express my deep, deep gratitude to Dr. Randolph Nugent, general secretary of the General Board of Global Ministries, who has believed in me and constantly supported me. I extend my thanks to Bishop Woodrow Hearn, whose wisdom and tactfulness have inspired me. I am particularly grateful to Kenneth R. Lutgen, Jr., associate general secretary of the United Methodist Committee on Relief, who has created many charitable projects for Russia and the C.I.S. and who truly feels compassion for our long-suffering people. I am grateful to Roger Burgess, who encouraged me to write this book. And I express my gratitude to Hans Växby, bishop of the North European Conference, for his spiritual support from the very beginning, and his trust.

Special thanks must go to my father and mother, Paul and Raisa Istomina, who have done so much for our church and for me personally; to my husband, Sergei Burmenko, and my children, Julia and Paul; and to my sister Irina and her husband, John Gibson, who took care of my children during my work for the church and while I wrote this book.

My love and thanks go to Lucy Smolenskaya, who did not merely translate this book but felt it deeply. Working on it, we laughed and cried together. Lucy became my spiritual mother. As you read our book, you will feel her soul.

My special thanks to Jim Wood—a former marine raider in World War II—and his wife, Rosie, and to Calwin and Gaye Cranor for "adopting" not only my children and me but our whole family. My special love goes to Dwight, Gay, Jenny, Kim, and David Ramsey. Special thanks and love to Michael and Jean Carmichael and to Jack and Jean Bush and the Wesleyan class, who helped Dwight and me in many ways. My deep appreciation goes to Jim and Mary Waddle, and James Gillespie for their great investment in developing Methodism in Ekaterinburg. Great thanks to all other members of our sister church, Broadmoor United Methodist Church in Shreveport, Louisiana, especially to Mattie Lee Watson, Paul Merkle, Carson and Maureen Turnage, Larry Hiller, Jason Weimar, John Porter, Robert and Brenda Haley, and David Hochstetler. I am very grateful to my Baptist friend Richard Davis, who has given me his constant support and changed my sister's life, and to my Catholic friend Ann Jones, who supported early Methodism in Russia and helped disabled children. My deep appreciation goes to the Reverend Ginger Holland for her courage and faithfulness, love and trust. I am particularly thankful to all the directors of the General Board of Global Ministries, who welcomed me into their friendly family and provided so much help when I became a director for Russia and the C.I.S, especially to the Rev. Frank Dorsey and W. C. Smallwood.

I am deeply grateful to Mary Ruth Howes for her editorial ideas. Great thanks go to all the members, and especially the youth, of the First United Methodist Church of Russia, Ekaterinburg—my best friends and helpers. This book came into being because of their love, prayers, patience, and understanding. My staff let me travel a great deal and speak in different churches all over the world, as they ran our growing church themselves.

My best wishes and my prayers go to all Methodist churches in Moscow, St. Petersburg, Samara, Pushkin, Pskov; in Sevastopol and Kerch, Crimea; to the Korean Methodist Church in Russia; to Asbury United Methodist Church in Kansas City, Missouri; to the First United Methodist Church in Macon, Mississippi; to the Sevierville United Methodist Church in Sevierville, Tennessee; and to other churches and all good people in the United States and all over the world.

Lydia P. Istomina

CONTENTS

FOREWORD

L ydia Istomina's fascinating story brings the reader as close as possible to the triumph and tragedy of first-century Christianity. The story of Lydia's conversion, with the help of American pastor Dwight Ramsey, her subsequent struggle with her new-found faith, the impact upon her family and friends, and the reviving of the Methodist community in the Soviet Union are all told with sensitivity and insight. The reader is able to "feel her soul" as she opens her heart to the struggles of bureaucratic red tape and hostility to the Christian church.

This moving account not only portrays the struggles of beginning a new church in the face of resistance, but also allows the reader a rare glimpse into Soviet family life and the sacrifices that generations of Christians had to endure under the Communist regime. The freedom of movement and the privilege of religious expression—rights that Westerners so often take for granted—are hard-fought on a daily, if not hourly, basis, for the Soviet Christian.

As Lydia fulfills her vows as pastor of the new community of faith, she experiences the love and affection of American people and the dedicated church members who undergirded her faith journey and supported her with their prayers, presence, and financial assistance. As the community of faith takes hold she begins to experience other, more internal, forms of resistance and strife—namely, conflict within the Christian community. Of all places, there should not be conflict within the body of Christ, but this realization tests her faith and ultimately makes her commitment even stronger.

Ronald P. Patterson
Advent 1995

1.

THE LIGHT BEGINS TO DAWN

July 1990 in Sverdlovsk began with a heat wave. Lucky people on holiday could escape to their summer cottages. Those who were still more fortunate were taking in the salty sea air on the beaches of the Black, Caspian, or Baltic Seas. The rest had to stay in the stifling heat of the enormous dusty city, unable to find coolness either in the shade of the trees or inside the buildings devoid of any hint of air conditioning. Only in old mansions and some special areas of the defense plants was it pleasantly cool. Of course, the air conditioners in the plants worked for armament, not for people.

On Friday, July 6, I was eager to get away to the country, where my son and the other members of my family had already gone, except for my fourteen-year-old daughter, Julia. She had been invited to a House of Peace concert, where she would meet American teenagers—the first "live" Americans in her life, and in the life of our town Sverdlovsk, formerly Ekaterinburg, in the Ural Mountains on the western edge of Siberia.* Sverdlovsk—closed, restricted and, yes, provincial.

Did the Americans know, I wondered, that Russia is not just Moscow and Leningrad? After traveling for thirty hours in an overly hot sleeping car from Moscow, they would have seen a vast country and would find themselves not in tundra or dense forest, but in a nice and rather old town with theaters, museums, beautiful old mansions—and a

---

* Because of its many defense plants and the prison camps (gulags) in the surrounding area, Sverdlovsk was closed to foreigners until the end of 1989. *Ed.*

tragic history. But first, at the railway station, they would see sweating people with knapsacks and crying children and frustrated parents, all heading away for the weekend. And then they would board a bus that, not allowing them a glimpse of the city, would rush them to a pioneer (youth) camp, where they were to stay for nine days.

How does a person survive in a heat wave? Only by taking cold—and frequent—showers and baths, preferably every hour, at work, at home, in the summer cottage, and especially after a bus ride! My working day was over, and all I could think of was getting cool. But there was that concert and meeting with the Americans at the House of Peace and Friendship. *How can I manage to drag Julia off with me to the country?* I wondered. *I can't insist; she is fourteen—almost grown up now.* I've always tried to persuade her to accept my point of view, but I've also given her full freedom, saying, "It's for you to decide." So now I was in a quandary.

My thoughts ran on: *I can't leave her alone: all the other members of our family are in the country. Julia's never gone by electric train by herself . . . and how I hate going to this ambitious Sultanovs' mansion* (our nickname for the House of Peace and Friendship, where the family of a former Communist boss had installed themselves). The family "reigns" there: the husband is the director of the house, his wife always plays her Russian accordion and wears an artificial dazzling smile, and their daughter charms the guests by playing her flute. It's a house for the elite. And I never had anything to do with such elite.

After talking with Julia, who came by my office at the university, I made a decision: We would attend the concert and meet the Americans and then take the train to the country. The occasion called for taking a taxi and going home to our apartment for a shower. Feeling cooler, we returned to the university. We would go to the meeting with Julia's friend Masha, her sister Dasha, and their mother, Lena Stepanova, who had just returned from the United

States, where she had been studying for two semesters. She was glad for a chance to practice her English.

What luck, I thought, *to have had that cold shower on such a hot day, even if we had to rush in a taxi to the other end of town for it!* The poor Americans were not so lucky, I learned later. They had no bath–shower accommodations in their rooms at the camp. Exhausted by the heat, they had waited for six hours for the bus to bring them into town for the concert and meeting.

When their bus stopped in front of the old mansion, sunburnt, smiling—in spite of everything—teenagers and a few grown-ups spilled out. In the general commotion, the first person who approached me introduced herself as Ann Jones. But for me, talking was useless! I was so nervous, I forgot all the English I used to know. Lena came up to lend a helping hand, and Ann's attention switched over to her. I sighed with relief and went inside the building with the crowd. There it was cool, as in all old buildings.

When the concert began, those who could find seats occupied them. Most of the Americans ingeniously sat down on the floor—a custom we Russians, to this day, find rather unusual. Still nervous, I started upstairs to avoid the crowd—and the concert —and stood beside an attractive woman in a dark blue dress. Sure that she was a Russian, I forgot my nervousness and stayed to watch the proceedings.

The concert went on and on—it seemed it would never end. The balalaika and accordion, the flute of the director's daughter—every piece interspersed with comments interpreted by a woman in a rather indecent transparent dress and an amazing wig—all seemed to exhaust the guests. Some of those who were sitting on the floor had fallen asleep. My patriotic feelings were not outraged, even though I didn't know then just how tired the poor Americans were. I was tired myself, what with the performers' shouts and jokes and the loud music. Everything is good in good measure, but the concert organizers, it seemed, kept whipping up the action. Their shouts, stampings, and tappings were getting louder and stronger. At times the old building seemed to groan. But I couldn't leave. Julia was nowhere in sight. I decided to drift with the current and wait it out.

Finally the concert was over and there was a storm of applause. Everybody was delighted—and relieved. My neighbor and I reacted in the same way, which further convinced me that she was the mother of one of Julia's classmates.

The young people were beginning to talk and introduce themselves. I went downstairs to find my daughter and spotted her making personal contact with a number of the guests. An American in blue jeans and a checkered shirt made his way toward me, and I noticed a wooden cross on his chest.

"Hello," he greeted me, and looked attentively into my eyes.

Something like an electric shock seemed to shake me, leaving me thoughtful and puzzled. He had already passed by as I managed to answer, "Hello." But suddenly he turned and came back, to look deep into my eyes. I could hardly see his face for his eyes. They studied me, exploring closely, as if probing or taking a sample; they narrowed a little, creating small wrinkles around them; then they laughed, glad to see something. As his eyes widened, the magnetic field between us weakened just a bit and I could make out his face—but not in detail, and afterwards I couldn't remember his face at all. The eyes were so strong, they dominated the face. It was as though they had a life of their own, very deep and completely beyond my comprehension.

Again he turned to leave. Suddenly I was afraid I would never see those attentive, searching eyes again. But once again he came back. This time he asked my name and introduced himself: "My name is Dwight Ramsey." The name meant nothing to me—and suddenly it became everything: the precursor of a whole new world, the forerunner of a new self, of my new life.

Dwight began to talk and ask questions, giving me no time to become frightened. And without realizing it, I began talking English to him. I told him I worked at the university, that I had come with my daughter. Unexpectedly spotting Julia in the crowd, I dragged her away from her new friends and introduced her to Dwight.

"I want to present you with these symbols," Dwight said, and he gave us each a small fish. It took a great deal of effort to explain the meaning of this symbol that is of such importance to me now. Dwight had to draw an arc on the parquet floor with his foot as, in fact, the first Christians had done, drawing the secret sign on the sand. I kept nodding my head and smiling, glad to understand what he was saying. God only knows how I managed to understand anything.

Suddenly Dwight gripped my hand. "I want you to meet my family," he said, and pulled me over to the woman in the blue dress, my neighbor at the concert. She proved to be his wife, Gay, the nice woman I had assumed to be some teenager's mother. And mother she was—she had come to Russia with her three children Jenny, Kim, and David.

Forty minutes later, I abruptly realized that I was talking with people whose mother tongue was English, and I lapsed into silence. Words stuck in my throat. I forced myself to speak, and even tried to use sign language, but the result was only a confused and hoarse croak. Dwight showed no surprise, but tactfully tried to help me. And then he invited me to hear him give a sermon on Sunday. He had been invited to speak at a Baptist chapel.

Well, I never! So, he is a priest! I thought in shocked surprise. But it's just impossible! Beardless, without a cassock, without long, greasy hair—and in jeans? I had never seen the like. Of course, five years ago nobody thought such a thing was possible.

I found it difficult to part from Dwight Ramsey and his family. I forgot all about the stifling heat. The only consolation was the thought that I would see him on Sunday. Aboard the train on the way to the country that evening, my daughter and I kept laughing happily for no good reason. We interrupted each other, sharing our impressions, comparing notes. We were as happy as though we had just visited some new world and were eager to bring that world intact to our relatives, to share it with them, to make them feel the same joy. But that is as difficult as trying to make people experience pleasant reminiscences by means of somebody else's photos.

Back in Sverdlovsk on Sunday, I went with trepidation to the Baptist chapel to hear my first sermon. I was childishly horrified at meeting Baptists. Why this fear? It had stuck fast in me after I saw the film *Thunderclouds over Borsk,* in which sectarians sacrificed a young girl. Our teachers had warned us to avoid talking with old women wearing kerchiefs—sect members. We were to call a policeman, they told us, if we ever met such women.

But Dwight's eyes had won me over at our first meeting, and I would have gone to hear his sermon whatever the place. And I didn't come alone; my children, Julia and Paul, accompanied me. From the first moment of my conversion, I entrusted my children to the Lord.

The first sermon in my life . . . it evoked feelings more than true understanding. The interpreter somehow disturbed me. Not that I could understand the sermon without his assistance, but Dwight's eyes were talking and I was able to hear and understand because I wanted to. God was saying to me at that hour: "I've come to you because you've been waiting for Me. I always knew you, but you were not ready."

Tears of joy were washing grief out of my heart. The pangs of bitterness I'd been living with disappeared and I could breathe more easily, more deeply. I could even see more than I usually did. What was the matter with my eyes? Where was all that blinding light coming from? God's love, His grace, His sacrifice. What did I know about Him then? Nothing. Yet suddenly I seemed to have understood everything at once, in a twinkling. Since that moment, my life has no longer belonged to me, but to Him.

The sermon lifted me over stupefying fear and tiresome fuss. It purified me through the tears drawn by the words addressed to me personally and heard by me for the first time: "God loves you!" I forgot the past. Even the nasty feeling of resentment, which had stuck like a lump inside me after the talk early in the day with KGB* people, now disappeared. The KGB talk was inevitable in view of my desire to invite Dwight and his family to my parents' house for a visit. To do that I had to get a permit, which involved specifying my parents' names, address, places of work, and other details. But as I listened to the sermon, the unpleasant feeling that somebody was constantly standing behind me and watching me dissolved. And, as it turned out, there were no fears, doubts, or problems God couldn't cope with. Everything was in His power!

Also, I now had a Bible of my own! Just think of it—the Bible that was impossible to buy in those times! A Bible was presented to me and to all those who came to hear the sermon by the visiting pastor. In those times, when foreigners were permitted to bring to the Soviet Union only one Bible that belonged to them personally, Dwight Ramsey had managed to get permission to bring in one hundred Bibles!

---

* KGB—Committee for State Security (Komitet Gosudarstvennoy Bezopasnosti), is a sinister version of the FBI and the CIA. *Ed.*

Now I feel like laughing at those KGB people trying to guess the Methodist pastor's plans. No doubt, they were trying to find out why he had come to Sverdlovsk, of all places.

Dwight Ramsey had been dreaming of going to Russia for twenty years. The dream had been haunting him since his days as a student. What was it that was drawing him here? If I had known anything about God's call then, I would have called it exactly that—God's call. But I won't try to be clever and invent names for what was in the soul and heart of this American, who looked like a Russian, perhaps even like a relative of mine.

As soon as Dwight's family crossed our threshold, we began to find coincidences. My father and Dwight looked like brothers—the likeness was striking. Several months later, when I looked through negatives of photos I had taken, I could never be sure which of the two men was my father. Both Dwight and my father were leaders, both had been pilots in the past, both had written dissertations and given lectures, and both were proud of their families and adored children. Both were gifted and strong personalities. But there was one difference. One was a convinced Communist and atheist, the other a pastor and a true believer.

As ideological opponents, my father and Dwight began studying each other at once, trying to win each other over and doing it professionally. I keep out of politics, so I did not find their dialogue interesting, in spite of its extraordinary psychological acuteness, and I was soon lost in thoughts of my own. Looking at the two families, so different and, one would assume, so alien, I thought: *Why do we feel so comfortable together, so easy?* Our family didn't get along with other relatives, and we never shared our innermost thoughts, feelings, sorrows, aches, and joys with other people. Our immediate family was enough—a safe, magic circle. We were self-sufficient people. Why, then, this eagerness for personal contact, along with such confidence and trust?

My father's loud voice interrupted my meditation. "Raisa, bring three wine glasses of vodka, please." There was a pause after his words addressed to Mother were translated. It appeared that a few minutes earlier my father, Paul, had asked Dwight the question, "Do you believe in the Trinity?"

"Of course I do," answered the Methodist pastor, not suspecting any tricks.

"Let's drink then," said my father. "One, two, three . . ."

Following my father's example, Dwight drank three glasses of vodka at one stroke, surrendering himself to the Creator, for he had never in his life drunk even beer. But retreat was impossible while Paul was looking at him so searchingly.

Loud laughter swept away all the awkwardness, and we felt easier. We were like fellow travelers in a train compartment who know they have nine days to spend together. Everything that we had been keeping to ourselves all these years now found expression in words, gestures, glances, and smiles. We were suddenly talking after so many years of silence—about joys and sorrows, doubts and anxieties, disappointments and hopes—believing that we would never meet again. All conceivable and inconceivable boundaries disappeared. We forgot the interpreter, who could not follow the changing course of our conversation in which all those present took part simultaneously. The fear of personal contact with foreigners was discarded, and we mixed Russian and English words, sometimes using expressive (as we thought), but not always understood gestures.

When words failed, Dwight took his guitar from its case and opened his soul to us in music. His expertise amazed me. It was even more jarring than seeing this clergyman wearing jeans! *So, a priest is just an ordinary man! He is just like me and you. He can be approachable and friendly!*

"What is your attitude toward God?" Dwight asked my father at one point.

"I'm an atheist," Paul answered proudly.

I was disappointed. *Well, they are beginning debates again!* I thought. But Father suddenly jumped up, went to the bookcase, and brought out some large, thick, hand-bound notebooks that had belonged to my grandfather. Dwight heard an extraordinary story, almost a legend, about a Christian who had been true to God all his life, who had lived through the revolution and two wars, the collectivization and dispossession of *kulaks,** and the betrayal and repeated loss of what he valued most—and who still managed to keep his love for the human race and remain a surprisingly trustful man.

Dwight was astounded by what he saw and heard, and Father's face was beaming. "We are no fools either!" he said.

Listening to my father talk about his father, Ignati, I couldn't know that I would take the same path as Granddad: the path of pain and love, disappointment and discovery, sacrifice and external resurrection through our Lord.

I wanted to say so much that evening, if only a part of what I'd been remembering. I often caught myself thinking on several levels at once—first, second, third. As I listened to Father's conversation with Dwight, I went on with my sad reminiscences about Granddad and at the same time tried to decide whether I could entrust any part of my secret heartache to the dry and rather ironical interpreter. I tried to realize that soon the days of our unexpected meeting and friendly talks with Dwight would be over and we would return to our normal life again. It was as though I was again mentally writing the book that had been living in me for nine years, but had only found expression in short stories,

---

* A farmer characterized by Communists as having excessive wealth.

comic sketches, and notes (none published), as well as suddenly splashed-out lines I could not find any use for. I would jot down lines on paper only when someone seemed to jar me into writing them. When I read them later, I'd be surprised; they sounded as though someone else had written them. At other times the book just lived in my mind, reminding me that nobody was interested in my soul and I'd better not share my thoughts and experiences with anyone—to do so was both silly and dangerous.

What I thought and felt could not interest this extraordinary man, I was sure. And so I could not express myself at all. My resulting silence lasted for three days. But to be with this pastor became a necessity. That's why I was so glad to hear Dwight's lamentations over the fact that he was not allowed to preach at Moscow University, because I realized I could make his dream come true in Sverdlovsk! Truly, the ways of our Lord are inscrutable!

I had been working as an executive secretary for the Znanie (Knowledge) Society Board at the Ural State University for eight years. My job involved drawing up programs and finding professors to give seminars and lectures for engineers, teachers, students, officers, and even prisoners. But I was also to invite interesting people—like scientists, actors, singers, famous writers, politicians—to the university. Dwight Ramsey would be just another interesting person to university people. They've seen all kinds of celebrities, so it's difficult to surprise them. Still, I was in a flurry before the meeting I had organized for teachers and officials of the university came about on July 11, 1990, another sweltering day, while perestroika—reconstruction—was in full swing.

But to my surprise, things were going fine. I had managed to order a bus—free of charge—to transport the Americans. I had persuaded the dean of the university to receive Dwight Ramsey. I had convinced the regional television boss that the event was especially significant, and he promised to send TV operators and a journalist. It was not just that he would be televising one of the first Americans to come to our "closed" town, but this was the first pastor to visit us, a pastor of the Methodist Church—a group nobody had ever heard anything about!

Early on the morning of July 11, the bus picked me up to fetch my new friends. Now there was no turning back. We were an hour and a half late, we had a long way to go, the bus was old, and twice we lost our way. By the time we rushed into the university building along with journalists and an American TV crew who had come to the Soviet Union with the delegation, I was terror-stricken. *Will anyone come? What shall I tell all these people I invited, if they do come? What shall I tell those I have brought if there are no people in the hall?*

The hall was packed! But it was also stifling because of the heat. *Who will stand this torture for more than forty minutes?* University people like independence, especially concerning working hours, and particularly in summer. The only thing I could do was to tell them about the man I had met three days before and hope for the best.

To my relief, the meeting went well. Dwight talked simply, about God—or rather, not so much about God, but about us, people. He mentioned the Lord's name just a few times, but always with great reverence.

From the very first moment there was tense silence in the hot, stuffy Hall of Academic Council. Everyone, without admitting it, was waiting for an answer, for the possibility of wonderful changes—maybe this man is really in possession of absolute truth. It would have been so easy to alienate us, to make us shut ourselves up in our own shells. We were so fed up with empty talks and speeches, with florid and ornate phrases. Only God could have helped this American pastor find true words and a genuine tone of voice. Again I felt the mysterious ability of this Methodist preacher to reach each of us simultaneously. It was a miracle—to see strong, experienced people shed tears. These were people I knew and respected. Their tears meant that this meeting touched their hearts as it did mine. It was not deception, or oratory, or just an actor's trick.

The words addressed to us may have been interrupted by translation, but the unity of hearts and souls that was born that day was not broken. Dwight asked us if we believed that love was better than hatred, that peace was better than war, that forgiveness was better than vengeance. *Yes, of course,* everybody agreed inwardly. *How can there be any doubts? This is the truth!* But why do we live without following this truth? Why do we yield again and again to envy and malice and then suffer and repent and sin again, turning our life into a tangle with a hopelessly lost end? Who can heal? Where can we find understanding and forgiveness? Who will give us strength to live, if our disappointment is so great that we can never believe anything? Never before had I heard such a dialogue. Neither had any of the others present, I felt. That's why nobody left after Dwight spoke, but stayed to talk and ask questions.

"They say, life is like a zebra," a young woman said, looking at Dwight with hopelessly sad eyes. "Why then is my life like an endless black stripe?"

The answer was short and quite unexpected: "Don't you think that all the time you are going along the black stripe? Try to turn your life ninety degrees and take the first step."

Dwight knew how to take that step, I felt and, more important, in what direction. Suddenly, I wanted to tell him everything. I felt like a hurt little girl who would like this big and kind man to put his hand on her head to comfort her and show he understood. It was so pleasant to feel him looking at me when he needed assistance, though I didn't stop to think that only by force of circumstances was I singled out of this multitude of people. But I wanted so much to help him, to feel that he needed my assistance. *And,* I thought, *he does need my assistance here, in this new situation.*

That feeling counterbalanced my growing dependence on him and helped me keep my seeming independence.

Finally the meeting was over, but people didn't want to leave. I found myself mentally urging everyone out because Dwight's family wanted to visit us again. They were going to come to my parents' apartment. I'd have a chance to talk about myself at last! On the other hand, my mother was in shock. "How can I feed them?" she had asked when I proposed having Dwight and his family stay overnight. "Where will they sleep? You'll have to give me some time to get things arranged." So, however much I wanted to talk with my new friends in private, I was glad, for my mother's sake, that the people crowding around Dwight were not in a hurry to leave.

To give Mother more time for preparation, we went sightseeing to the site of the Ipatiev House, where Tsar Nicholas II and his family had been killed during the revolution. There were so many legends about the house, stories told in whispers when I was a little girl, that the house had been blown up, so that people would forget the tragedy. But with glasnost and perestroika changes had come, and advocates of justice were inspired to erect an Orthodox cross to mark the place of the execution. The cross made passersby stop and bare their heads. Flowers were placed in front of the cross. And newly married couples, who had formerly been in the habit of visiting other sacred places such as Lenin's monument, now began coming here as well.

Periodically, the cross was destroyed. Patiently and persistently it was erected again. I had never suspected there might be such a deep-seated political struggle going on in the town. Now, seeing some of its outbursts, I tried to keep aloof, not trusting either side.

When we finally arrived at my parents' place, I took a look at my brave mother's smiling and affable face and knew that with her true Russian resourcefulness she had managed to come out of the situation with credit. Nobody suspected how much effort it had cost her to prepare food for all of us!

After supper we talked and laughed a lot. Then a number of us went for a walk around the beautiful and now deserted central part of Sverdlovsk. Returning home, we stood in amazement, looking at our small boys, David and Paul, who had gone to sleep together and were lying in identical poses, sucking their thumbs. The silence of these moments, full of love and trust, united all of us for life, telling us more about one another than any words could ever do. The two children, an American and a Russian, were trustfully snuggling up to each other, and we could feel love for our children conquering all fears and doubts. Seven of us spent the night in my parents' two rooms.*

In this new confidence, we still had disquieting questions. Who told Dwight the truth he knows now? How and when did it happen? Who helped him come to God? Questions raised other questions, and time was alarmingly pushing us toward the date we were afraid to think about— the Americans' departure. To get as many answers as possible, we tried to spend every moment together, so much so that David Stone, the head of the American delegation, was quite upset with Dwight, who often broke the delegation's timetable so he could spend more time with his new flock.

Problems were being solved in my parents' apartment, but nobody could imagine their importance then! Dwight was trying to find out through my father the rules and procedure for founding a Methodist community in Sverdlovsk. Father, with the assistance of Misha Saburov, our interpreter and my daughter's teacher, was trying to get all the necessary information. As for me, I had no idea how

---

* The seven were my mother and father, myself and my son Paul, Dwight and Gay Ramsey, and their son David. The girls, Julia, Jenny, and Kim, and my sister Irina, spent the night with our acquaintances Larisa and Anatoli Arshavsky.

deeply involved I would become in all this, because I knew nothing about Dwight's plans.

The day after we all had spent that night at my parents' apartment, I began to speak English without realizing it, until Gay, with a sly smile, remarked, "Lydia, it appears you know English." I suddenly felt like a secret service man taken unawares when trying to conceal his knowledge of English. But Gay's tact and inborn sense of humor helped me cope with my sudden confusion.

That day there was an official reception for the American delegation in the Hall of the City Soviet.* I felt quite out of place there. Who am I to be present here? I wondered. So I remained in the reception room, but through the open doors I could hear everything. After the greetings and an exchange of presents, according to protocol, it was Dwight Ramsey's turn to speak, and he addressed the city administration: "I've got a dream . . ."

Dwight's request for the Political Education House, the Communist propaganda center, to be assigned to a Methodist church was met with a roar of laughter, breaking all the polite restrictions of official receptions. People thought Dwight was crazy. No man in his right mind would have dared in those times to bury the Communist Party this house belonged to. But that's what Dwight was doing, because he thought this attractive building in the central part of Sverdlovsk was already vacated!

Receiving no permission to found a religious community, Dwight made another request: "You've got public organizations of writers, veterans, scientists. Why not permit an association of Methodists?" So, an official permission form was obtained, and Dwight began collecting the required twenty signatures.

---

* The equivalent of our city hall, the meeting place of the soviet, the city's "elected" (that is, for their lifetime) officials. *Ed.*

While our American friends were in Sverdlovsk, some odd incidents occurred that seemed to indicate that the authorities were keeping close tabs on them. One evening some university acquaintances of mine invited Dwight and all of us to their apartment. Dwight and my sister Irina stayed on overnight after the party. They were to come the next morning to the pioneer camp where the American delegation was staying, and we would meet them there. When I drove up to the camp, I was stopped by vigilant KGB men.

"Do you know what term of imprisonment you may get for speculation in icons?" they said peremptorily.

I was flabbergasted. *Icons?* Since my grandparents' deaths I had never had a chance to hold a single icon in my hands. What was going on? But the men's aggressiveness wasn't letting up. Fortunately, at that moment Dwight appeared on the stairs and explained the situation. After I had left the party the night before, my university acquaintances had presented Dwight with an icon. Though no one besides Dwight, my sister, and the hosts had been in the house, when Dwight came to the camp the next morning, everyone there knew about the icon!

The Americans' last day in Sverdlovsk was marked by another incident, both odd and somewhat frightening. Dwight was eager to see the building of the former Voznesenski Cathedral, which at that time housed the Museum of Regional Studies, but he had told none of us of his plans. Several of us had been standing near the House of Peace and Friendship for a long time, talking and saying good-bye, when Dwight suddenly suggested going to the cathedral. Victor Peretolchin, an old schoolmate of mine, drove us there. Just as we reached the parking area, a gray Volga passed us in a hurry and parked in front of the cathedral. A youthful, rather stout man in a sport suit jumped out of the car and ran to the church building, pressing his hand to his right pocket.

My heart missed a beat, and I had an unpleasant cold sensation in my stomach. Were we just imagining things? No other people were near the museum except for a slim young man reading a book. The stout man ran up the steps into the museum, and a little later ran back down the steps. Then he began to saunter, as if taking a walk. He stopped near the young man, talked to him briefly, and then disappeared.

Dwight and Victor went to the museum while Victor's wife and I remained in the car. When Victor and Dwight returned, Anatoli Arshavsky and my sister Irina were with them. They had gotten to the museum a little before we did and had also seen the two men. Dwight, Victor, Anatoli, and Irina had not been admitted into the museum. Through the closed door, an elderly woman had told them that the museum was closed for the day and that she was alone in the building and was afraid to open the door. Fortunately, I happened to have with me a certificate attesting that I worked in the Znanie society of the university. So I invited Dwight to try again. After long explanations and negotiations through the closed door, we heard the metallic sound of the bolt being turned. Very slowly, the elderly woman opened the door—and when we looked beyond her behind the little old woman's back we spotted the two men!

After that experience, we all rushed to my apartment to get something to eat. But we began to sing and to talk, forgetting about food. Then Dwight invited all of us to stand up, and he began to read the Bible aloud. The longer he read, the more I understood that he was reading for me and about me. He was reading the story of the first woman Christian in Europe—Lydia! As I listened to the account of Lydia and Paul, my body felt frozen and I began to shiver. I felt that God had prepared a special road for me. What was it? Where must I go? I did not know. I only felt in my soul: *This is the moment to come to a decision.*

There were twelve of us: my sister Irina, my husband, Sergei, my school friend Victor, my children, Julia and Paul, my friends Larisa and Anatoli, Nina, Lena Stepanova, and her two girls, Masha and Dasha, and myself. (There was a thirteenth person present, Victor's wife, Tatiana, but she was frightened and not ready to make a decision, so she waited in another room.) The twelve of us decided to become a Methodist association. And I was elected the leader of the community. (Later, when we were alone, Irina said to me, "You'll be put into prison! Think about the children!")

Thus a Methodist community in Sverdlovsk, the first such community in Russia since the destruction of the Methodist church in St. Petersburg in 1934, was founded. We didn't know anything yet about Methodism, and we knew practically nothing about Christ. But we were sure of one thing: we wanted to be together. God united us through the Methodist pastor He had sent to us.

2.

THE PARADOX OF GROWING UP RUSSIAN

Personal History

Writing about oneself is never simple. A person runs the risk of meeting the mocking glances of acquaintances who suddenly know one's innermost thoughts. We Russians find it difficult to "strip" ourselves in public, to share our emotions and sufferings. It's just as difficult to open our hearts in happiness and cry from the housetops about our love and joy. We'd rather show restraint, because we are sure that nobody is interested in our feelings. Unless one happens by chance to share the same sleeping compartment with a stranger whom the person is certain he or she will never meet again, that person may never have an opportunity to share his or her life history.

I'm in no way different. I'd feel easier—and much safer—keeping my confidences to myself. But after meeting Dwight Ramsey, I felt an urge to speak about myself, to understand what my "I" really means.

My "I" embraces many people and things: my grandfather, who gave me so much, my parents, my sister, my husband and children, my few real friends, my town and—I'm not afraid of seeming emotional—my country. I suppose people have to talk about themselves. If we don't, we'll lose our history, our past, which is rather like a stained-glass window—a wonderful picture made up of thousands of multicolored pieces. One piece of stained glass can't remain in place if it isn't supported by the other pieces. So when we relate some seemingly commonplace story about ourselves, we are also, perhaps unwittingly, talking about scores of other people. We, like the piece of glass, can't exist without the others. Otherwise the unity, the Creator's plan, is upset.

As I look back, I can see that, in truth, God had plans for me, even from birth. When my mother was pregnant with me, she suffered from a serious heart disease. All her doctors insisted that she terminate the pregnancy. Thank God my grandfather intervened, or I might not have been born. He was a true believer and trusted that our Lord would preserve both mother and child. Determinedly, he took up his stand in the doorway of the house, not letting my mother out. His words have become part of our family history: "Don't be afraid, Raisa! We'll help you and bring up the baby, too!" Those words can be found in the book my grandfather kept writing throughout his life about our family.

My parents had a hard time of it with me. To begin with, Mother's pregnancy lasted ten months instead of nine. During childhood, I had several illnesses and infections. I was afraid of the dark and terrified of being alone. If my parents had to leave me alone, I would cower stock-still in the corner between the door and the wall and would breathe quietly, trying not to be seen or heard. Sometimes I would actually go to sleep standing there. This shallow and quiet breathing remains a habit to this day. After we got married, my husband, Sergei, used to wake up at night in terror and call my name to make sure that I was alive.

Mother had nicknames for me, like "the sly one" and "the quiet mouse." Unlike my sister Irina, who was a smart and noisy imp, I was taciturn, uncommunicative, buttoned up and, at the same time, capable of any act. Even at the age of two, I took offense easily and nursed a grudge for a long time; when my offender had long forgotten about it and never expected any tricks from me, I would react. At that age I didn't so much plan my revenge—it was just my nature. After committing an offense, I would hide under the long, fringed cloth covering the dining room table. I'd sit

33

there, dreaming: "I'll go away to some very distant place so that my parents will miss me and will be sorry!"

While she was very young, my sister began to write poetry and to draw; everything she did was a success. Mother hoped I would be a painter—I heard her whisper that when she saw me looking at reproductions of famous pictures. That was something I would do for hours. Reality somehow faded into the background, while the smallest details of the picture became clear, the finest and most imperceptible touches and shades sharpened. I was amazed when some new figures suddenly appeared in a well-known picture, formed by interlacing branches, crosses, lines. However, the day I overheard her whispered remark, my concentration was interrupted and I lost all sense of mystery—and any desire to continue in art.

As I teenager, I was disgusting! I was lazy, impertinent, and always ready for a fight. I always felt inferior to others. My sister and I went to the same school, because there was just a year's difference between us. Mother was director of studies at our school, so wherever we turned, there was control. Our teachers, who taught many subjects, often said to Mother, "How different your children are! Just heaven and earth!" My sister was heaven, naturally, I was the opposite. I could read for hours, especially Russian fairy tales, but it was so dull to do homework! When I did do it, I tried to be clever: out of five problems I solved the first, third, and fifth. I also tried to follow this rule when doing calligraphy exercises, copying paragraphs from a Russian story. But once, when I was to write just one sentence, I wrote in my copybook the first, the third, and the last word!

At school we had to wear ugly brown uniforms, but my parents wanted to see me dressed differently, so they bought me a blue dress. From then on I was labeled "an imaginer," and my classmates would bite me. I did have an imagination, and my stories irritated them as well. Finally, I couldn't take the bites and teasing and I asked my parents,

"Please buy me a uniform. I really want to be like all the others!"

My first teacher was a very kind woman who always petted me and said I was her best pupil. Once we had a written test, and after checking it, she said, "All those who got a five [the highest mark] stand up!" I stood, and it appeared I was the only one out of forty pupils to get a five! Four students got a four, ten got a three, and the other twenty-five got unsatisfactory marks. It was such a joy to talk about my success! But after a success, we suffer even more when we fail. The results of the next test struck me dumb. I expected another triumph—but I was the only pupil to get a bad mark.

During my first year at school, my parents had to buy me four schoolbags, whereas my sister had the same schoolbag for five years! I would leave my bag in a shop while I was lost in contemplation of whatever was on display. Once, my grandmother found my bag in a shop a week after I'd been there, but by then I was already sporting a new one.

There's no telling what kind of person I would have become if it weren't for a strange sensation I began to have, as if someone was watching me. I experienced this sensation at the most unexpected moments. After I read *Gulliver's Travels,* I could easily imagine a giant playing with our planet as if it were a toy, and I tried to live in such a way that I would be worthy of his attention. And what's more, I couldn't lie, because he would immediately expose me. Thanks to this sense of being watched, I stopped doing things that could be denounced by people. I stopped being lazy, envious, rude, and cruel. In this I was assisted by the Voice, which I heard for the first time when I was twelve. It took me in hand, when I needed it badly.

I first heard the Voice one day when I was feeling depressed and hopeless. It began as a vibration. At first it was frightening. Then the vibration ceased, and I began to hear a strange language. Without understanding the words, I somehow grasped the essence of the message. The monologue was unemotional and monotonous, but the force of what it was suggesting grew, as did my anxiety that I was doing something wrong.

The Voice would take me unawares when I was doing homework, or trying to shirk washing dishes. Try as I would to ignore it, I could not! The force of the Voice became so great that I was never able to do anything that would divert me from my duty. But as soon as I began doing what was necessary, the Voice of conscience left me, and I understood that I was doing the right thing.

I never told anyone about the Voice. The sensations of this struggle were far from pleasant. Then after two years the Voice disappeared, and I just forgot about it. I only remembered this experience a year or two ago while preparing one of my sermons.

My Grandfather

Growing up, we were told by our parents to respect our elders, to help the weak ones. But more often we heard, "Don't be good to people and you will not know any harm."

We used to sing in school about being "masters of our boundless motherland." In actuality, we were humiliated and oppressed from childhood on. We were humiliated little by little: standing in long lines at shops with numbers written on our palms; purchasing butter, flour, and sausage with coupons. We were allowed to buy only two kilos—4.4 pounds—of meat a year for every member of the family, and then only before the "revolutionary" holidays, November 7 and May 1, making us, as I used to say with a jeer when I began to understand things, "strong enough to drag our feet as far as the Square and shout a 'Hurrah'!"

Of course, many people had enough strength, even without the meat. We had a version of socialist social justice: we all had equally little, and all got whatever else they could wherever they could, and if they could not then the more foolish they were! Peter the Great's saying was part of our culture: "If you are hiring a cook, don't pay him more than sixty rubles. He will steal the rest of his salary." The ironic jokes of the famous humorist Michael Zhvanetsky were in vogue: "What I guard, I have. If I guard nothing, I have nothing!" Another saying was, "What belongs to everyone really belongs to no one." So bright Russians kept carrying "nobody's property" to their flats and country cottages. One day the ancient cobblestones were wrenched out of the pavement in front of the Sverdlovsk Opera House, where they had been lying for two hundred years! In exchange for a bottle of vodka, three truckloads of cobblestones were moved to my college's summer cottages, along with some old (but not antique!) furniture from the university—though I suppose the same could also have happened to antiques.

The Russian people are intuitive and possess a wonderful sense of humor. In our minds we formed pictures of life in foreign lands. Though we never saw any foreigners in Sverdlovsk, and the one and only TV program in those times could give us very limited information, we "knew" almost everything about them. We were adept at reading between the lines. When a second TV program appeared some years later, we laughed at the verbal "pearls" dropped by local politicians and announcers, and at the appeals for "harvesting battles" in the potato fields! Every year we were called upon to "display fortitude and conscientiousness" in the face of some natural disaster. The announcer's voice would be anxious and solemn, a little sad and austere. After such an appeal we all felt as though we were seeing that poster of our civil war times: "Have you registered as a volunteer?" The gloom seemed to be endless. Only a few people knew the truth: that mismanagement and laziness, hard drinking and bribery were flourishing.

I often wondered how Granddad, offended and humiliated thousands of times in his life, had contrived to keep his tolerance and purity, knowing and seeing the truth. But even he once asked: "For what did they make this revolution? People are the same beggars they were before!"

There were three main ingredients of my grandfather's life: true faith in God, hard work, and a dream about his book. Granddad left this life quietly, as if he were saying good-bye and parting piece by piece with everything he held dear. He spent his last five years in the same room, on the same sofa, staring at the rough, whitewashed wall. He would lie there and not get up at all—not because of illness, but because he didn't want to get up; there was no longer any point in his living. The walls of the comfortable, warm log house he had built fifty years before had been pulled down. But he had not been back to see the disfigured, ruined dwelling it had become. Nor had he seen his former neighbors digging among the ruins, looking for things he couldn't take to his new small flat. His last strength had been spent on parting with his two bird-cherry trees just a week before he had to leave his home. The trees had grown with his children. He had planted them just after he came to Sverdlovsk, thus marking his place on the land. Only after that did he begin to build his log house.

When his oldest daughter insisted that my grandfather, Ignati, leave the house and move to an apartment for her benefit, he decided to destroy everything himself. He could not bear the thought of strangers tearing down his house and everything around it that had been part of his life. But he managed only to saw down the bird-cherry trees; after that there was no strength left in him. And he lost his memory.

It would be a lie if I said Ignati had admired those trees for their beauty. Peasants' love is practical. Every August, Granddad would tie a large container on his belt and slowly climb up the strong branches. He had to climb high: the trees were almost fifty years old and he could no longer reach the fruit-bearing branches, even from the top of the longest ladder he had. His grandchildren would screw up their eyes in horrified admiration, watching in silence, waiting for him to climb back down with the lustrous berries lightly powdered with summer dust.

It was our family tradition to preserve the berries for winter; we dried them or ground them with sugar, pits and all. On holidays, my grandmother, Macarina—no one used this old-fashioned name; everyone called her Nina—would take hot, sweet pies with light crusts and bird-cherry filling out of the Russian stove, and the fragrance would fill the house. When we ate them, the ground-up pits would crackle in our teeth.

Ignati never stored more berries than necessary. After he had picked what he needed, he would call the neighborhood kids and they would climb up and settle in the trees for a long time, picking and eating. One can't imagine how many of them came on those cherry-picking days. And if Granddad happened to have a spare moment, he would stare up at the trees, lost in reverie, and then look around at the cherry-stained urchins scurrying through his yard.

Granddad's memory associated his log house with many things: hunger, war, persecution. He had not moved to Sverdlovsk of his own free will. He grew up in the little village of Podyelnik (which means, "under the fir trees"), near the town of Krasnoufimsk, west of Sverdlovsk. But in the Stalinist collectivization of the late 1920s and the 1930s, he lost everything—house, land, horses, cattle; he had not even been allowed to take his clothes and bare necessities from his own house. "Church man," the accusers called him. That label was enough to bring persecution. They also called him "Kulak!" He was no kulak—no wealthy, exploitive landowner—just an industrious one; but the label stuck, and it sealed his fate.

On that terrible day in February 1928, my grandmother had been in labor in the bathhouse, and when she finally dragged herself to the porch with the newborn son in her arms (her fourth child, my father), she found the door boarded shut with two boards nailed crosswise. A few people with red bands on their sleeves—her own villagers—were waiting for her.

I shall not describe my grandmother's feelings on that day, though I certainly know what they were. All the words in my book have to be absolutely authentic; I don't want to invent anything. So I'll say only that my grandmother took an axe, came up to the porch, knelt down, and laid her head on the steps. "Chop my head off," she told the villagers. "I won't be able to rear the children."

Granddad often told me a story about his neighbor in Podyelnik—an idler and a drunkard. I liked the story, but its true meaning came to me only after Granddad's death.

When Ignati went haying, he would harness his horse and call to his horseless neighbor, "Ivan, get ready! Let's make hay." Ivan, lying in a drunken stupor, could not even mumble a reply. So Granddad cut his own hay by himself. But his peasant's heart didn't give him any peace until he finished cutting the hay on his neighbor's plot, too. And so it went all summer long, year in, year out. Ignati cut, raked, and turned Ivan's hay, then stacked it for him. When snow came, he hauled Ivan's hay in from the field to Ivan's shed.

Years later, I read in Granddad's book that it was Ivan who, after becoming one of the "activists" in the village, had deprived Granddad of his home and had stood over my grandmother on the porch steps.

Granddad obeyed the commandment, "Love thy neighbor as thyself." Because of him, I have come to understand the tragic and deep meaning of this commandment.

Granddad told us a lot of stories from the village and from his early days in Sverdlovsk. "Oh-ho-ho-ho" he would sigh, usually after a long period of silence. Then the grandchildren would know he had remembered something interesting from his past. We would immediately settle down beside him near the stove, fighting for the place closest to him. I was his favorite and as often as not found myself at his right side. We would sit on our haunches all evening listening to Granddad. His low, beloved voice would merge with the crackling of the resinous wood and the smell of the stove and imperceptibly cast a spell over us. Sometimes we would doze off, lulled by the greedy, furious fire behind the red-hot stove window. When we came to, Granddad would be finished: "Oh, how hard it was . . ."

In Sverdlovsk, Granddad used to sit on a bench under the bird-cherry trees every evening after work. People going by invariably stopped and greeted him. Talking with my grandfather was extremely interesting. Though he had attended parish school for only four years, he was quite an educated man. He knew a lot of verses by heart, had read a great deal, and always respected and envied people who knew foreign languages. He was a true Russian intellectual. His speech was clean and simple, his soul was not burdened with grave sins. (Even during World War I, he never killed— he just shot his rifle into the sky.) That's why it was pure joy just to be with him.

Although I didn't know it when he was alive, Granddad was also an active member of Christian meetings that were held in secret. He observed all the rules of conspiracy. Fearing he might lose his Bible during a search, Ignati several times copied out a good portion of the Holy Scriptures by hand, as well as hymns. He kept those books, which he had carefully bound himself, in a metal ammunition box under his bed, along with his sermons.

The thing Ignati valued most was the Bible that had once belonged to an Orthodox priest, a relative, who was killed during the terrible time of reprisals. The Bible was leather-bound and had metal locks and very beautiful pictures, each covered with a thin transparent paper leaf. We grew up with this Bible without understanding its true meaning, or our good fortune in having it, but only feeling some trepidation when we watched Granddad perform the same solemn ceremony each time he opened it. He carefully spread a newspaper on the table, then washed his hands thoroughly before taking the Bible out of the metal box. Only after he had prayed for a long time did he begin reading. We children were strictly forbidden even to touch this hiding place, but as soon as Granddad left the house, we immediately dragged out the heavy box from under the bed, to look at and read the Bible, which attracted us because of its inaccessibility and mystery. I think now that Granddad did it on purpose. He was a wise man: "Forbidden fruit is sweet!"

The bench under the trees and the Bible are interconnected in a strange way. Once, when Granddad was sitting on the bench, he was approached by a bearded stranger who got talking about his dream of entering seminary and becoming a priest. In those times, that was next to impossible. People talked about churches in whispers. Yet there, before Granddad's eyes, was someone who wanted to be a priest! The only difficulty was that the young man had no Bible. My grandfather brought out the most valuable thing he had—his Bible—and gave it to the stranger. Whatever the relatives said, railing at him afterwards, Granddad's answer was short: "That was a man of God." And even when a policeman came later on and informed him that the young man had been detained in Moscow when trying to sell the Bible to foreigners, my grandfather remained blissfully calm. He was convinced that the lad needed the Bible more than he did.

In His mercy, God took away Granddad's perception of time during his last years. It seems to me now that Granddad was getting ready for this loss all his life by painstakingly, in his peasant's way, writing down every event in his book, which he dreamed of seeing in print and holding in his toil-hardened hands.

Toward the end of their lives, my grandparents were moved to a tiny flat, where they were locked up in their room by their oldest daughter and her family, who didn't allow them to leave the room without permission, even to go to the bathroom or the kitchen. A slop pail was placed in their room, as well as a thermos with hot water. Other relatives were unaware of these conditions, for a semblance of well-being was contrived, so that when they came for a visit, the door was unlocked and open. Grandma had been intimidated into keeping silent, and we never suspected anything wrong. Only when she neared her death did she begin to complain.

During his last years, Granddad had only his memories of the three houses he had built. The houses were gone, as were the trees, the bench, and the yard where he made and repaired things. There are no trees with a bench under them, no house, no yard where he can make and repair things; there was no work to be done; there was no sense in living. There was only a whitewashed wall for him to stare at, and a stain that grew wider with each day, created by Granddad himself. All his life he liked carpentry, and he had a habit of holding nails between his teeth. Little by little, a sort of erosion appeared on his lip, which eventually became malignant. Granddad found a way to alleviate the constant irritation and pain; he would moisten his finger with saliva, touch the wall with the wet finger, and smear his lip with the lime. That was how the large round stain appeared on the wall over his head.

Five years with the widening stain. Five years alone with his thoughts, a heavy heart, and deep mortification. Grandfather died with a sigh, asking for a drink of water but failing to take it. He died without explaining to me the true meaning of the command, "Love thy neighbor as thyself." He died, leaving me his books and an unceasing heartache: why couldn't I do anything for him? He died, leaving the enormous round stain that kept coming through the new whitewashing as a bitter reproach to us all.

Religion

As a young person I knew practically nothing about Christianity, or about how to have a relationship with God. However, I felt closer to God on a mountain than anywhere else. Here I was helped by my father, who taught me to love mountain climbing. On a mountain, I became myself, free to talk rather than being shut up in my own shell. I could talk with summits for hours. I liked this conversation—respectful on my part, the voice of the Creator so simple and majestic.

I didn't know much about churches, either, but every time I happened to be in some seaside town, I would go to the church. There I would be wonder-struck and find it difficult to leave. As soon as I got into the cool silence of the church, I had only one wish—to fall on my knees and pay homage to God's grandeur. In my hometown, Sverdlovsk, I only went to church a few times: people going to church got onto "lists." Mother, a believer at heart, had never been to church. But I used to be sent to accompany Granddad when, having lost his memory, he would lose his way in our large city.

The spiritual atmosphere of our home mixed strangely with what we were taught at school. It was quite common, though, to hear teachers who taught us that there was no God exclaim now and then, "Thank God!" When we heard about Yuri Gagarin's cosmic flight—the first man in space—there was no end to our joy. Almost immediately a short song appeared about how this flight proved the absence of God and showed all believers the absurdity of their faith:

Gagarin proved the earth was round
And there was no God around!

Shouting these words, we dashed into Grandma's house and began jumping around her, repeating the verse. Grandma tried to make us stop and looked around for Granddad. Granddad, who had never laid a hand on us or even touched us in anger, now banged me so hard on the forehead with a wooden spoon that he drummed the truth into my head forever: faith as well as old age must be treated with respect and reverence.

Every Sunday Granddad and Grandma went to the church. I would still be lying in bed when I would hear Granddad's boots stamping down the stairs—we lived on the fifth floor. Granddad didn't like modern clothes, and to his last days wore trousers tucked into tarpaulin boots and a Russian shirt belted over the trousers. Seeing Granddad on the street from afar, we would rush to meet him, squealing, hugging, and kissing him, while our classmates, who were usually ashamed of their older relatives, looked at us in perplexity.

Every year before Epiphany, Granddad brought holy water from the church and sprinkled all the corners of our flat. I remember how earnestly he fasted during Lent: he ate only bread, vegetables, and vegetable oil—no meat, fish, butter, milk, or eggs. But he was very lenient with us. Feeling pity for him, I would secretly add sour cream or butter to his soup. Then, with sinking heart, I would wait: *Will he guess my secret?* His eyes would narrow. "What kind of soup is this?" he would ask, smiling into his mustache.

"I don't really know, Granddaddy. Grandma cooked it," I would answer, hardly moving my lips. I knew Granddad hated lies.

At Easter, Mother dyed eggs with onion husks and baked an Easter cake. In the morning she woke us up with the sacred words: "Christ is risen."

"He is risen indeed," we would answer, kissing each other three times, as Russians do.

Eggs were dyed and Easter cakes baked in every house, but nobody talked about it. Moreover, our parents asked us to tell no one about it. The morning after Easter, my classmates seemed embarrassed. It was as if we all had experienced something important and mysterious, but nobody wanted to admit it.

"Those who ate dyed eggs yesterday, raise your hands," our teachers asked. A forest of hands rose in every class!

We talked about atheism, but at every step we said the words, "O Lord," "Thank God," "Lord, help me!"

God in My Life

Our church came into being in defiance of the prevailing conventional notion. It aroused suspicion, laughter, irritation, and bewilderment. My persistence made some people shrug their shoulders. Others simply and impudently twirled an index finger near the temple: "Clear as day—she is not all there."

In the opinion of many, I sold myself for dollars—my price being $25 a month! I know how much a cleaning woman is paid for tidying an apartment: $35. For lawn mowing the pay is $45. Such work takes two to three hours at most. So I have not sinned in this.

O Lord, You chose to change my fate. You made me meet Dwight. It was Your will to make me face people whom I never trusted, when I preferred to manage my life without their hypocritical friendship. In my life I have met a lot of mean and treacherous people. I know what made me believe them again and again, and keep on being sadly mistaken.

You know, Lord. You alone know how things were with me before You came to me.

Before the summer of 1990, I was half alive. I wanted only to be left alone. *It's safer this way,* was my thinking. *No one will make me angry, or trample on my trustfulness, or defame me.* I held my honest name so dear. Though I tried to be obedient, I was becoming timorous. I betrayed the brave, independent, wayward and pure child that I had been, so that I could be like all the people around me. But I failed again. I was unable to bribe or be bribed. I couldn't kowtow to people I didn't respect. In spite of my gentle disposition, I couldn't play the hypocrite and keep telling a fool that he was clever. Sooner or later I dropped those people, lest I would have to call them in their presence the fools, rascals, and thieves that they were.

The process of change began with my son.

In 1985 I had been looking forward to the birth of my second child, wanting to use the time to hide from people, to wait, to be alone, to read and think, to understand what I was and why. After my son's birth, I felt younger than I was. Braver. More confident. I felt I could do anything. At this time in my life I did seek the Lord's guidance. But that was soon to change.

When he was twenty months old, Paul had an attack of convulsions and his temperature suddenly shot up. I lost my head and could only cry, "Paul, don't die; Paul, don't die." It shames me to write about my behavior in the next hour.

For forty minutes I tried in vain to telephone the emergency service. The emergency operators rather coldly advised me to call the doctor on duty at the children's clinic. However, it was a holiday period and nobody wanted to take the call. All that time I was in another room, forgetting how my son needed my presence. Then something made me return to Paul's bed. Suddenly he gave a start, and then his little body went limp and his chest did not rise anymore. Sobbing, I grabbed Paul and began to shake him so that his little head bobbed from side to side, but nothing helped. I laid him on the bed and opened his eyes. His eyeballs were rolled back, and he wasn't breathing.

Then something in my brain cleared up. *Time! Has it been less than five minutes since his breathing stopped?* I began to give him artificial respiration. It seemed as if somebody were telling me: *Tongue! It could have rolled back! It's necessary to clear the gullet.* I began to do what was necessary. My fingers gripped his tongue and pulled at it. I heard a whistling inhalation and then such a frightened cry that I could hardly bear it. Paul looked as if he had just been in some very distant place. For a long time after this he was unable to smile.

I believe God tried to show me the way to Himself, not only through my son's illness but also through my own illness.

Paul had not completely recovered from his illness when I developed a strange sickness. My body shook with awful fits of trembling until I was sure I could no longer endure the pain, or the terrible fear. It seemed to me I was in the terminal stages of an illness for which no doctor had any help. I was having six to seven attacks of shivering a day and began thinking of myself as an invalid. In my mind I said good-bye to everything I held dear, including my son, who was still ailing.

Where am I at fault? I wondered. *What sin is God punishing me for? How can I find out?*

One day, I decided to go to the Russian Orthodox church, St. John's, right after work, just as I was, wearing my usual makeup. In the church, though, I felt out of place. I couldn't understand what I was expected to do. I knew only that people usually lit candles—but where should I put them? Suppose I made a mistake and put the candles for the dead where those for the living were supposed to go. *God forbid!* So I went away. Then I thought of singing in the choir—but I didn't know how to go about it or where to apply.

Finally I began praying at home. If my son went to sleep early, I had a few moments left before leaving his room. Those were the moments when I prayed and talked with God—a naïve and primitive, but frank talk. Right then I needed no one as much as I needed the Lord. But I understood and knew nothing about Him. Only later did I understand that my painful attacks of shivering were His attempts to talk to me, His attempts to teach me. But I was too frightened at the time. I just thought I was dying.

God was taking care of me, but He didn't show Himself in all His might. I came to know Jesus step by step. (Once, much later, I even saw Him.) After I was born anew, everything found its place. I had another Teacher, one whom I had known since my childhood. Thanks to Him I was born. Thanks to Him I had heard the Voice of conscience when I was an ungainly and wayward teenager. Thanks to Him I met Dwight, made new friends, discovered that old enemies could become friends, and was reunited with relatives I had not seen for ten to fifteen years.

3.

BIRTH PANGS: THE STRUGGLE TO BECOME A METHODIST CHURCH

Getting the Signatures

Sometimes when we receive a present we wonder what to do with it. I felt just like that after Dwight's departure: overjoyed at what had happened and confused as to the future.

"You'll be put in prison, Lydka," my sister whispered to me as soon as Dwight's car drove away from our house. I was shivering again, just as I had when Dwight had read about Paul and Lydia from the Bible (Acts 16:11-40). My thoughts were all in a jumble—not because of fear for myself or even for my children. It was rather from diffidence. *Why me? Will I have enough strength?* The devil of doubt took hold of me and was trying to destroy the fragile temple that had so surprisingly risen in my soul: *Who am I? What can I teach? Who will believe me?*

All these thoughts insistently led me to one conclusion: Lena Stepanova must be the leader! She knows the Bible, she speaks English. True, she used to teach atheism, but . . . (Three years later Lena confessed to me how tortured she had been by the question, "Why didn't Dwight choose me to lead? Why Lydia, not me?")

My diffidence was not only genuine but, I thought, realistic. The Bible presented to me by Dwight Ramsey was my first step toward knowing the Scriptures, if you don't count my childish experience with Granddad's Bible. But my associates assumed that because I had been elected the leader of our community, I certainly knew the Bible and had already been initiated into the sacramental secrets of faith.

I felt like a puppy thrown into a pond with only two options: to swim for life or to drown. I was fortunate because our Lord took me into His embrace. But right at that moment I only knew that I had to swim for life. So I began by looking for someone who would be a "real" leader of the church, one who believed in God and knew the Bible. Thus my first step was made away from myself.

My job at the university gave me a chance to meet different people. One whom I respected most was Daniil Pivovarov, a doctor of philosophy, a true intellectual and a decent person. So I went to him with my proposal. Of course I was upset and disappointed when I heard his gentle refusal. I had wanted so much for our community to be led by this experienced and religious man from the first days of its existence. Only much later did I appreciate his tact and foresight.

Our first meetings took place in the office of the University Communist Party Committee! Not officially, of course, but only because I had access to the key. It sounds funny, but history is history. These meetings looked like anything but prayer or church meetings. We did not know how to pray. We were not even allowed to pronounce God's name in that office. But neither could we have started in any other place, for two reasons. First, there was a powerful barrier of embarrassment and bewilderment in every one of us; there was not a single Christian of longstanding among us. Second, any gathering of believers, as officials "kindly" explained to me on behalf of the powers that be, "may be conducted in the form of meetings, but without prayers or singing." Our meetings would have looked like the sittings of the Party committee itself, had I known how to conduct one. Unfortunately, or maybe fortunately, I had no experience in either. What helped me overcome my inner timidity before our meetings? I felt a sense of responsibility for our future Methodist church begin to sprout in me, though I knew practically nothing about this church.

This feeling of responsibility appeared after I met Vladimir Tomakh, a tall young man who came to my office just after Dwight's departure. Vladimir wanted to enter the Management Institute that we had organized at the university. While telling him about the institute, I suddenly began to talk about the Methodist Church. Thus, I think, I began serving our Lord. I remember how inspired and joyful I was to find Vladimir a very attentive listener. The task facing our community at this point was to get an official registration. Nobody had ever heard anything about Methodists. But the pulse of our life was beating already. There had to be more of us. People had to learn about us; we had to find more supporters and sympathizers.

Vladimir made this task the goal of his life. I gave him the original of Dwight's address to the city administration, and he left with it, promising to return several days later. While I waited anxiously for his return, I wondered why I had handed him the only document given to me by Dwight. I could not answer that question then. Three days later Vladimir returned in a state of euphoria. He had spent those days on holiday talking to different people, friends and strangers, telling them about the Methodist Church and Dwight's idea of building a church in our town. The document now was signed by sixty people!

At that moment, looking at those sheets of paper with the names, addresses, and signatures of sixty people I did not know, I suddenly understood that those people were my vocation. *To sign any document and give one's address was a tremendous act of courage.* Though they knew nothing about the Methodist Church and Methodists, these people wanted to support the new movement. Their desire was far from being faith yet. In fact, not many of them joined the movement and became Methodists. Their signing could have meant many things: perhaps they were sick and tired of the gray monotony of our dismal, and in many respects limited, life.

Whatever made people take this step, the number grew from day to day. By September we had 602 signatures. It could never have happened without God's providence. Regrettably, Vladimir became famous as a man obsessed with the Methodist Church. Many people laughed at him, and with his characteristic ardor he got into an argument and landed in the hospital. Knowing nothing about his tragedy, I lost touch with him for a long time.

The second step to get the church registered could not have been predicted. I went to Moscow to meet Boris Yeltsin in person and show him the list of signatures. Yeltsin was at that time head of the Russian Federation Supreme Soviet.*

This insane idea could have occurred only to Dwight Ramsey; yet it didn't seem insane to me.

I didn't even ask myself why I was going to Moscow. My main concern beforehand was finding money for the trip. Never had I been so brave. I went to my boss, Aphanasi Kuznetsov, a historical writer, and asked him to send me on business to Moscow.

"Where, exactly, are you going?" he asked

"To the Supreme Soviet," I told him honestly.

My boss was struck dumb, and I got the money for my airplane ticket!

I never doubted for a moment that Yeltsin would receive me. I knew, of course, that I would look funny to Muscovites—like "a messenger of truth from the Urals." That was the description that used to be given to any person from

---

* Yeltsin was born in the Urals and managed a construction company in Sverdlovsk before he was appointed Sverdlovsk's Communist Party's First Secretary in 1976. In 1985 he was called to Moscow to supervise construction in the whole of the USSR for the Central Committee, and became a member of the Politburo. In 1987 he resigned from the Politburo in disgrace; but in 1989 he managed to get elected to the new Congress of People's Deputies from Moscow with 89 percent of the vote! In May 1990 he was elected chairman of the new Russian Supreme Soviet. *Ed.*

out-of-the-way regions who came to Moscow to see Lenin. But I also knew that my cause was right. "Our cause is right, the victory will be ours" was what we had been taught since childhood. It was only when I walked up to the Supreme Soviet building—the white house that was to become so famous in October 1993, three years later—that I understood just how silly my venture was. At the gate I was stopped and questioned about my invitation and pass. With no invitation, but also without any doubts, somehow I won! I was inside, and the magnificent elevator was taking me up to the floor where Alexander Tsaregorodtsev, one of Yeltsin's assistants who was also a former citizen of Sverdlovsk, had his office. And there all wonders came to an end. Even God retreated in the face of the Soviet bureaucracy!

"What do you expect me to do?" The tall man with a pious, inexpressive face appeared irritated by my request and gave me a puzzled rather than a surprised look. Obviously I didn't deserve surprise. I was just some crazy woman from the Urals, hoping to see Yeltsin personally.

"There are many pastors," Tsaregorodtsev pronounced at last in a weary voice, "but there is only one Yeltsin."

"How can you say that? Are there really many pastors?" I replied indignantly, and began to defend the pastor who had changed my life.

"The audience is over." The words interrupted my monologue in defense of Methodism and its only representative I knew so far. Leaving the Supreme Soviet building, I walked along Kalinin Prospekt, weeping bitterly. For the first time I felt lonely: along this new path I must do everything myself.

Near Old Arbat, I saw a crowd of people and wondered what was happening. From afar I recognized Boris Yeltsin and Mikhail Gorbachev. *Good gracious! What a chance!* I thought. Then as I pushed through the crowd, I burst out laughing. They were cardboard figures of both leaders, put up for the benefit of anyone who wanted to have their pictures taken with the leaders. There were a lot of volunteers.

Then I was struck with a naughty idea: Why not do the same and bring the fraudulent photo to Sverdlovsk? And I did. Many people afterwards examined the photo with surprise, unable to believe that Yeltsin in the picture was not real. When I look at this photo, it reminds me of my naïveté, my courage, and my impotence.

Soon after my return, a frightful tragedy happened in Moscow. Alexander Meyn, an Orthodox priest, was murdered on the way to his church on a Sunday morning. Why should Father Alexander be murdered so brutally and with such cold-blooded premeditation? To find the reason, I tried to read everything I could about his murder. I found and bought Meyn's books, *The Human Son* and *Herald of God's Kingdom,* and after reading them fell in love with the author.

People must be right when they say that the Lord takes the best people to Himself, I thought. *But whose hand could have dared to strike this priest? Aren't the wild times of repression over, when thousands of priests were shot, tortured in prisons, and sent to perish in Siberia? What, then, about Protestants?*

I admit that in September 1990 I was frightened, thinking of the dangers for myself and for my family, even though I was not a pastor then, but only an unknown leader of a tiny Methodist community. But being proud, I never told anyone about my fears. "If you pledge, do not hedge!" the Russian proverb says. Once you've begun, you can't back out.

And here I shall mention an incident that occurred four years later. All through those four years I had been trying to buy as many books by Alexander Meyn as I could. It was very important for me to read his books. I wanted to follow the course of his reasoning. That man was pure and had a spark of God, indeed. But my attempts to find all his books ended in failure, and I wondered why. Then I received a sharp reply to my request from the attendant in a bookstall of Orthodox literature: "There are no books by Meyn and there won't be any!"

Another shop assistant, a young man who looked like an ascetic, answered me gently: "Father Alexander had some serious doctrinal mistakes, so his works are prohibited now." Just like that! The man is no more. There are no books by him. There are no problems either.*

This was the familiar peremptory shout: "Not allowed!" How much all of us lost because of it in the past. We were deprived of the right to choose. We could read, see, and eat only what was permitted. That is probably why Soviet people had such a great power of imagination. We had nothing left but to be proud of the little we had. We were doomed to learn by heart: "Soviet people have a pride of their own; we look down on the bourgeois and the rich!"

Why are we always afraid of the truth? Why are we afraid in general? The most terrible thing is that we all keep silent, isn't it? We all have kept silent for seventy years. We've all kept silent about seeing priests murdered, churches and books burned, the best of men persecuted. Unfortunately, Meyn was not the last victim.

The Struggle for Registration

Our church was registered on October 24, 1990, as "The Methodist Church Community." The day before the registration was to be discussed by the City Soviet Presidium,* I had to coordinate the last details with the City Soviet lawyer and a head of the City Religion Committee, Maya Mikhailova. These usually nice and kind women were

---

* Alexander Meyn (Aleksandr Men) had not cooperated with the KGB under Brezhnev, but had taught secret Bible classes. For the two years or so before his death he had been preaching openly on radio and TV. *Ed.*

* The Presidium is the administrative governmental committee that acts when the Soviet, the legislative council, is in recess. *Ed.*

unusually aggressive and distrustful. They greeted me with the angry reproach: "You are only going to register your community, aren't you? But you have already got the land for the church building!"

I'm always taken aback by impudent attacks, as are most people, I suppose.

"What land?" I asked in amazement. "Have they already given us land?"*

"Stop playing the fool!" Maya snapped. "You have managed, behind our backs, to get the best plot of land in the city, to stir up public opinion. Tomorrow the city newspaper will publish a letter of protest against the Methodist church. Scientists and leading actors of Sverdlovsk are going to picket roads leading to Vainer Park."

Vainer Park, named after a local Revolutionary War "hero," was quite a popular park when my parents were young. A brass band played there in summer, and our citizens danced and had a good time in the evenings. It was now neglected and overgrown with weeds, but the town patriots were going to stand up staunchly for this historical heritage! I was embarrassed and perplexed by the accusation—because I didn't understand it. I only knew that, though guiltless, I was guilty!

Was I a Methodist? Yes!

Was I developing the church? Yes, I was.

Was I going to receive the land? Apparently so!

Well, there is the evidence. The sentence of guilt is passed without right of appeal. Suddenly I understood: There will be no registration. There will be no Methodist church.

"Please, stop the article, it's a mistake," I whispered, hardly able to check my tears.

Maya Mikhailova exchanged glances with the lawyer, and I sensed their thinking. *Maybe there really is some kind of*

---

*Land isn't bought in Russia. Land for any building project has to be granted by the city or state government. *Ed.*

muddle; she sounds quite sincere and even flabbergasted. They phoned the journalist author of that malicious and unverified article, and I explained everything to him, trying at the same time to get from him how this extraordinary turn of events occurred.

It seemed that a quick-witted and enterprising citizen of Sverdlovsk, a certain Urmanov who was a frequent visitor at the Supreme Soviet in Moscow, somehow got hold of Dwight Ramsey's original documents, which had been sent by the Peace to the Children of the World Association to the Supreme Soviet addressed to Boris Yeltsin. Mr. Urmanov was the representative in Sverdlovsk for the Center of Assistance to the People's Deputy B. N. Yeltsin,* and he brought these impressive documents, signed by the governor of Louisiana and by Bishop Oden, to the head of our town. He took it upon himself to explain Dwight Ramsey's idea of building a church in Sverdlovsk and expressed the readiness of the center to participate in this project. Yuri Samarin, head of the town at that time, took Mr. Urmanov for the representative of our community and wrote on this document: "The Center of People's Deputy B. N. Yeltsin. I ask to work up the question of defining the place and further steps. Yuri Samarin. 9/25/90." The very popular center was given the most attractive plot of land for construction.

After I talked to him, Urmanov actually talked to Dwight Ramsey about the proposal to build a Methodist church in Sverdlovsk. That put Dwight in a dilemma: Should he develop the church with inexperienced novices, whose leader had no backing or connections, or should he say yes to enterprising politicians who were ready to realize the pastor's dream in the shortest time? Though the temptation was great to go the quick way, Dwight chose me. It took him just one day (which in those times seemed quite

---

* Roughly the equivalent of a campaign office or home office of a senator or a member of Congress in the U.S. *Ed.*

impossible: we had no fax, and only a few people in the whole city had one) to send a document to me from Louisiana, certifying my rights. Thus he decided to take a long and far from simple path to his goal.

Our community had a difficult meeting with the leaders of the Center for Assistance. Red-haired, freckle-faced Urmanov, who had stolen the documents from one of the tables in the Supreme Soviet Secretariat (the legislative building), tried to stall us in order to hush up the growing scandal and to prove to all of us that he had acted for our own good and had intended to make us a present of the church after it was built. Then came a belated offer of cooperation. The idea of developing the church by building it with the support of experienced politicians was very alluring. But we refused. We wanted to do everything ourselves and, most important, to do it with clean hands.

In spite of the journalist's promise to the contrary, the article did appear in the town newspaper, *The Evening Sverdlovsk,* under the spiteful headline "Setting the Axe to the Old Park." Actually, one didn't have to read the newspapers to be aware of the fact. On the streetcar, I heard the indignant passengers reviling "those Methodists." The citizens, united by "noble impulses" and heated by "patriotic feelings," expressed their thoughts vigorously—but hardly decently.

Good gracious! I thought as I listened to them. *What am I doing? I don't know anything about the Methodist Church yet! What if this church should bring misfortune here?*

At that point I saw that my vocation was not only to bring Methodism to Russia, it was also to help it develop, remembering our roots and without wounding the "mysterious Russian soul." And then I thought of Granddad. *How would I have told him about the Methodist Church?* I wondered. I suddenly realized how important it was for us to find some Methodist roots in our country.

I started by asking Father, to his surprise, for the old notebooks left by Granddad, and I began to look through them. I read with interest about Granddad's family buying an American harvesting machine in 1912—the only one in their village. I was amazed that Granddad had also had some contacts with Americans and had thought highly of their technology and machinery.

When I read about secret prayer meetings, I was surprised. I hadn't heard about them before. When I asked him, Father told me that Granddad not only had been the Orthodox believer I knew him to be, but also had been a member of a Protestant sect. The Orthodox church wasn't enough for him. That's why he attended the secret meetings and tried to express himself through his own sermons. Eventually Ignati was condemned by the leader of the sect because he had not turned away from the Orthodox church. All his life Granddad kept patiently trying to find his church, but something was missing.

Perhaps it was the Methodist Church Granddad was looking for! I thought, startled. I did find in his notebook some mention of Methodism, but I can't place too much emphasis on it—it was just mentioned in passing. Still, rereading those old notebooks somehow eased my inner tension: Granddad would have understood and supported me! I felt he would have been happy that I had come to God, and I wanted my grandfather to be proud of me. From then on, one of my aims was to make our church hospitable for such people as my grandfather.

The day after the article appeared, our fate was decided at the City Soviet. In spite of the scandal, the church was given official status and the right to open a bank account. Now we could take up the issue of getting the land. *The First United Methodist Church of Russia!* And it was in Sverdlovsk that it was born!

Later on, when we had to register our church in accordance with the new law of Russia, we finally got the right to this name. Still later, when we had to drop the word *Russia* in order to avoid paying monstrous taxes, the fact did not change the essence of the matter. We were and remained the first United Methodist church in Russia. I used to joke afterwards: "Russians are very modest. Now our name is not 'The First United Methodist Church of Russia,' but simply 'The First United Methodist Church'—of the whole world!" Believe me, joking was necessary. Humor was often my only salvation, at times the only support when I needed it badly.

In the weeks that followed, not many people came to our meetings, though there were new members. Ludmila Vaschekina joined our congregation, then her daughter Marina. When Ardo Rennik, an Estonian, joined our community, he helped me find fellow Methodists in the USSR. There was a Methodist church in Estonia, he told us. Through his brother, he also found out the telephone number. When I heard the calm, soft voice of Georg Lamberg, the pastor of the Russian Methodist Church in Estonia, I could not help crying for joy; we were not alone now. While we talked, his daughter Marika began playing the piano and singing "What a Friend We Have in Jesus."

Soon after that, a stranger telephoned to introduce himself: "I am from Georg Lamberg." Through him I got a copy of the charter of the Estonian Methodist church, my first piece of religious literature. Later on I got a copy of *The Book of Discipline,* as well as my friends' letters, books, and more Bibles—all through "hand-to-hand" Methodist mail!

When it came time to receive the land, another trial was in store for us. At the sitting of the city council, Deputy Goncharenko suddenly shouted hysterically that I was trying to stir up a second Ulster in the Urals (war between Protestants and Orthodox). The rest of the deputies, accustomed to their colleague's rude manners, nevertheless got to thinking: *Let the land go to waste rather than give it to Americans!* The issue was put to the vote, and the majority of deputies voted against the motion.

When someone is up against a brick wall, there is a slight possibility that he or she can break through it. But here I had no hope whatsoever. For I wasn't up against a wall. I felt as if I were sinking in quicksand. A feeling of impotence and hopelessness gripped me—the more I struggled, the deeper I sank. I can't stand shouting in general, but it's especially offensive when people yell and insult in public. But there was more to come.

Another woman from the Religion Committee of the City Soviet, Tatiana Tagieva, invited Vladimir Victorov, one of the most competent scientists from the university and a former KGB officer, to the next sitting of the people's deputies so he could tell them about the Methodist Church. The sitting was again accompanied by the implacable Goncharenko's shouts and loud remarks, and the head of the City Soviet had a hard time controlling him. The scientist tried to bring home the main idea: the Methodist Church is a peaceful church; it never waged war against anybody.

In spite of a separate brisk address in defense of the citizens' patriotic feelings and against the dangerous invasion of Protestants, "Comrade" Goncharenko failed to win his point. The general heated discussion was suddenly interrupted by the unusually calm voice of an impressive-looking deputy: "As a matter of fact, why all this noise? One would think, looking at you, that the Methodist Church was going to bury nuclear waste in the center of Sverdlovsk! It's clear that it only wants to build, with American assistance, a religious center which, by the way, could beautify Sverdlovsk and become a new center of culture!"

Embarrassed, all the deputies fell silent. Then they began the voting. This time, we won!

Led by the Light

Just before Easter of 1991, I decided to go to Leningrad. During one of our telephone conversations, Dwight had put me right, telling me that we had not brought Methodism to Russia—we were reviving it. His words made me start reading, but the literature I could find on the subject was scant. My main source of information was the third volume of *The Dictionary of Atheism,* under "Protestant." The few articles I did find were not enough and, frankly speaking, frightened me a little. In one of them, I saw a photo of wild-looking people in a state of religious ecstasy, with the author's commentary: "The Methodist preacher brought the parishioners to madness and made them extremely nervous. After such sermons many fell down in convulsions, others were unconscious or trembling and screamed shrilly for hours." I did not show this article to the members of our community!

It was after that when I decided to go to Leningrad to look for the truth in the city's archives. I felt that the Methodist Church was congenial and right for us. But some Protestant sermons and services made me uneasy. Every Sunday on central TV we heard Jimmy Swaggart's sermons. His programs reminded me of festive shows. That kind of church could never suit Russian people.

When I boarded the plane to Leningrad, I was alone with my thoughts for the first time in months. The rapid succession of problems and events and my work in three organizations simultaneously in order to earn more money (my husband was seriously ill and not able to work, while my expenses for international phone calls were growing from day to day) had left me no time for thinking, or for getting in touch with myself. As a result of that trip, I learned to love airplane travel. For a short time airplanes provide a state or feeling of complete freedom. It's like being in some intermediate or interstitial state: between past and future, sky and earth, friends and new acquaintances. For a short time I belong only to myself. I like to travel unaccompanied. On board a plane, unexpected revelations sometimes come to me, as one did that day, while the plane was still climbing.

At first I fell asleep, it seemed. Then suddenly I saw people in white garments, of different ages and appearance. They looked like ancient Roman sculptures, but they were living people. They appeared, then gave place to others, saying nothing. For some reason I scrutinized their faces as if I were looking for someone.

Then, I saw Him! Jesus! He was thoughtful, not sad, and He was looking at me attentively, studying me. I thought perhaps I was sleeping, but my eyes were open. I began to weep, but Jesus didn't disappear. Then I was afraid. *Jesus has come to take me away. These are my last moments. Jesus doesn't come for no reason. It's impossible just to see Him. I must be dying.*

Part of me really did die. The former shy and timorous Lydushka—diffident, full of complexes and fears—died at that moment.

Tears streamed down my face, so many that they washed away all doubts, all pain. I sighed deeply. And then I saw the frightened eyes of my neighbor. I could only smile. It was impossible to explain my experience. The whole thing was a miracle. I was miraculously born for the second time. I came to know Jesus and was baptized by the Holy Spirit.

From that time on, I truly began to pray. I could speak with the Lord, knowing the One whom I addressed. In one short, heavenly moment, Jesus gave me knowledge and wisdom, His light and His truth. From then on, every time I prayed, a column of light touched my inclined head. Words can't describe the color of that light. This wide, shining, milky white ray of light lifted up my prayers and gave me strength and support. Often, too, while praying, I felt Christ touch my shoulders, as though He came up behind me and blessed me. Listening to Him, I learned to be meek and humble.

Through that experience, God taught me to trust Him completely. That was just what I did. I gave Him both myself and my children. When I left the plane, I was quite a different person—now I was just the way God made me.

During my time in Leningrad, I learned how little a person really needs to get along: a bed for sleeping, a table for working, and a chair for sitting. (I remember Granddad saying, "You can't sit on two chairs—it's too uncomfortable!")

In this beautiful and spiritual city, I began to see that I had a responsibility to make the story of Russian Methodists known to people. I wanted to attract the attention of the best and most honest scientists to the history of the Methodist Church in Russia.

I found some of the information I was looking for in the Museum of Religion on Nevski Prospekt. The museum had been created in the old Kazanski Cathedral. (Across from the cathedral one could visit a swimming pool inside the beautiful Lutheran Church of St. Peter and St. Paul.) I was standing in front of the display devoted to Protestants, examining photos and church relics of Baptists, Lutherans, and Adventists, when I glanced up and saw on the wall the name "Methodists." But there was no information concerning Methodism under it, just the word. But that meant there had been Methodists in Russia once. *What could have happened to them,* I wondered, *so that only their name was left in the museum?*

I found a research worker and asked her to help me get permission to work in the archives. Irina Simonova, a tall, slender blonde woman, agreed. After going through all the formalities, I went to the depository, where I could look through old journals and magazines. I had never been lucky in the past, but now I had entered new time when dreams came true and everything turned out well. We succeeded in finding copies of a journal published by the Methodist Church from 1910 to the present—*The Christian Advocate.* I also found copies of the first Methodist hymns translated into Russian.

But the thing I value most, I found in the old journals—a sheet of paper covered with writing in pencil. The text was written in 1923 by one of the leaders of the Methodist Church. I figured it out after finding the names of Sister Ann and Bishop Burt in the text. With the research worker's permission, I took the sheet home with me to keep—nobody at the museum needed it. It helps to imbue me with the spirit of those times, when the Methodist Church still existed in Russia.

At last it became clear to me what I must do. I must tell people about leaders in the past whose souls were pure and who tried to teach others; who consistently taught, healed, preached, and cared for the poor and orphans, without letting up and without sparing themselves. My task was to help people learn to give more than to get. But it is not easy to teach that to people who haven't had enough for generation after generation, who have dreamed only of a better life for their children. It is not easy, either, to teach that to people who are ready to give away everything at a difficult moment, even to sacrifice themselves for others in a disaster. The question is, what about the rest of the time? As one of our humorists said, "You need disaster to make people kind, but in good times people are like wolves."

In that connection, I remember a story I once read in our local newspaper about an older woman who was dying of hunger in her one-room flat. To the right and to the left, above her and below her, were neighbors, but none of them, it seemed, could find five minutes to knock at her door and find out if she was there, if she was alive. When there was no food left in the apartment, the woman lit a burner on the gas stove, switched off the electricity, lay down on her bed so she could see the flame, and waited to die. Perhaps the flame helped her forget her loneliness or helped her to pray. So she died.

A year later, someone asked the people in the apartment house, "When did you last see this woman, your neighbor?"

The neighbors sent for the police. When the door was broken down, they were horrified, but not by the tragedy or even their own callousness. They were horrified by the thought that all of them could have died if the gas had spread through the building! "The house might have exploded!" they said. Only later did any of them feel embarrassed because they thought first of themselves.

All of us had gotten into the habit of being indifferent. While thinking about achieving "great victories," we had gotten used to passing by the poor, the lonely, and the deprived. Was it because all of us were equally deprived? Perhaps.

In order to follow my vocation, I needed great strength. First of all I had to be sure that I understood my calling correctly. After my unhappy experience with St. John's Church in Sverdlovsk, I knew I couldn't go there for answers. But in Leningrad, I decided to try the Orthodox church again. First I went to the Cathedral of the Blood. Seeing the splendor of this sacred place, I was disturbed. *Maybe my place is in the Orthodox church after all,* I thought, and my doubts stirred again. I recalled my talk with my fourteen-year-old daughter, whose opinion I valued. Julia, for whom the beauty and mystery of the Orthodox church were very important, could not accept the Methodist Church. It seemed to her that Jimmy Swaggart's buffoonery was what a Methodist service really was. As for me, I had no information and personal experience to help her feel the spirit of Methodism that I accepted. *Perhaps my daughter is right and I am in error,* I thought.

Greatly perturbed, I went to the Isaak Cathedral. From a childhood visit I remembered the enormous pendulum hanging in the center of the cathedral. This time, the cathedral seemed less like a museum. By intuition—for I knew nothing then about the peculiar force of the center in the cathedral, which is outlined by a circle—I rushed into the center and turned to face the altar. The golden doors of the iconostasis were wide open, and I could see the altar and behind it Christ rising in brilliant light in the magnificent stained-glass window.*

The sight of the glorious risen Christ spoke to me of the mystery of the second birth. It settled all my doubts. I had my answer: Methodism is the path I must follow. The stained-glass window can coexist with the Orthodox altar just as Methodism can coexist with Orthodoxy. The Orthodox roots and traditions of Russian believers will enrich Methodism. Methodism will help the nonbeliever get to know Christ and choose his own church, whether Orthodox or some other. Methodism has always had educational tendencies. Maybe the purpose of the Methodist Church in Russia is to educate the people, to help them choose the right path of faith, and then to give them a chance to decide for themselves.

The Lord gave me generous gifts that day: I stood in the center of the Isaakievski Cathedral and torrents of light, love, and forgiveness streamed down on my head. Unable to take my eyes off Jesus, I felt His closeness, His support, and His blessing.

---

* Isaak Cathedral is a unique Orthodox church in that it has stained-glass windows. The iconostasis is the screen, or doors, in front of the altar. The doors are usually closed to hide the altar from the view of the worshipers. *Ed.*

4.

THE NEED FOR THE METHODIST CHURCH

The Need for Tolerance and Understanding

*I*n the subsequent events of 1991, I began to see clearly why we need Methodism in Russia, and why it has begun to revive just now, in my time. For one thing, the Methodist Church teaches people to be tolerant, understanding, and accepting of differences.

Tolerance—that is just what we in the former USSR lack. Reared on the milk of collectivism, most of us had become intolerant and cruel individuals, trained to teach and propagandize what we didn't believe ourselves and to condemn anyone who didn't conform. Now, on the threshold of approaching bloodshed, we needed something very calm and stable. The Orthodox church might have become such a peaceful refuge for us. But we began to read newspaper and magazine articles exposing Orthodox priests, calling them policemen with holsters under their robes. The stories did us an ill turn. Many of us forgot the thousand-year history of Christianity in Russia; we forgot the many thousands of Orthodox priests who had perished for their faith after the revolution.

In 1990, all kinds of faiths had begun to collapse: faith in Communism, in Lenin, in the ultimate victory of the USSR, in the Great Patriotic War,* in Soviet public health services as the best, in internationalism. Nothing could fill the emptiness left in our souls. Besides, we were afraid of being deceived again.

---

* The Great Patriotic War is the name Communists gave to World War II (1939-45) and the fighting in various places in Europe that preceded it (1937-39), e.g., in Spain. *Ed.*

"A drowning man will grasp at straws." That could describe the country from 1989 to 1991. During this turbulent period, the country sat gaping at TV screens, thirsty for both information and entertainment—and hoping for a miracle. We watched the magician-psychiatrist-healer Anatoly Kashpirovski from Kiev in the Ukraine, who promised instant recovery for all suffering people in the Soviet Union. The lame, the blind, the disfigured, those who suffered from serious illnesses, even people seeking a cure for problems such as baldness or nighttime incontinence—all were mesmerized by Kashpirovski's voice. Every evening they sat in front of their televisions to be "treated" by this healer. However, their deceived souls went on aching.

Another healer, with the expressive name Chumak (*chuma* means "plague" in Russian!), convinced many people they could be healed by drinking water "charged" through the TV set. Every morning these people filled containers with water and placed them near their TV sets so Chumak could "charge" the water with healing properties. People drank this "charged" water, hoping to get rid of their ailments.

Being trustful by nature and frightened by my children's illnesses, I watched those TV programs, though I did not set out any water for charging, fearing that my husband, Sergei, quite an ace in electronics, would think me silly or even stupid. Even so, I once ventured to ask Sergei, "What if there is really something there?"

"What is 'there'?" My husband repeated the question with some irritation. And hearing no answer from me, for naturally I was unable to find the words I needed, Sergei whispered sarcastically, "I know how this box is constructed. There is nothing there and there cannot be!"

My young son Paul, seeing Kashpirovski's face on the screen, hid behind the sofa and cried that he didn't want to look at that "uncle."

The country also watched the sittings of the USSR Supreme Soviet deputies, which began to be broadcast on

TV in 1989. Everyone was glued to their TV sets trying not
to miss a single word. We used to say, "The country sits
staring at 'the box.'" The box, by the way, was rather
bulky—to the detriment of the screen, which was very
small—and could not withstand overheating. Some political fans who sat in front of the television set all night
became unintended victims of the political arguments
when their TV sets caught fire. Everyone, young and old,
waited to learn heretofore unknown facts about the horri-
fying history of the October Revolution, the Great Patriotic
War, the KGB. The country was eager to know its "heroes,"
real and imagined.

Who is to blame? That age-old Russian question was on
everyone's mind during those days.

Watching the historic battles of deputies, which sometimes turned into real fights, diverted people from reality.
The new life, marked by a frail democracy, provided another kind of narcotic—an illusion of participation in what
was happening. As if anyone could solve even one problem
while sitting in front of the TV set! But, no doubt, our
preoccupation diverted people from barricades and demon-
strations for quite a long time. We listened to the witticisms
of seemingly educated people: "I spared no effort so that
invalids could sit in this hall," declared the USSR Supreme
Soviet chairman, Anatoly Lukyanov, at one of the con-
gresses. "We do not have sex in Russia," said a woman
deputy. "We wanted to do the best and got it as always,"
stated another deputy. "The main thing is, being," said
Mikhail Gorbachev.

Russians and Work

Practically no one worked during the broadcasts of the
Supreme Soviet sittings. People didn't want to miss a single
word. After each session they spent time in heated discus-
sions. Actually, it hardly mattered that no one worked,

because salaries almost never depended on how one worked on the job, nor did bonuses! This principle never suited me. I was always a *rara avis*. I loved working and never could just idle away my work hours. I would rather do all my work in four hours and then go home to my daughter, even though I would be paid only half of what others were getting for sitting idle all day. "If you have nothing to do," I used to urge other women, "why don't you go home and take your children from the children's 'incubators'"—our overloaded state kindergartens.

"Of course, it would be nice," replied one of my colleagues. "But then my husband will make me do all the housework. And now I'm at my job, just as he is, and earning just as much." Yes, there was a deep feminine wisdom in that reasoning.

Earning some extra money by taking a second job was basically prohibited in those times. No one was allowed to hold two posts at the same time. (Many people did, however.) Only teachers could have several jobs. I knew that, not merely by hearsay; my sister and I grew up with our parents seldom at home. Both of them—as teachers— worked in two or three places in order to break away from poverty and to live a little better. Every summer, instead of taking a usual vacation, they went to work in children's camps so they would have enough money to take us to the Black Sea.

My parents never learned how to take a rest. People like them are called "work fiends"—workaholics. Mother planned carefully for her summer "vacation" at the children's camps so she wouldn't have a single free day at home! She came to this practice by trial and error, after having several "nerve attacks" on her days of doing nothing. The nervous stress that she thought would have burnt itself out in the whirlpool of regular teaching in several places overtook her on her free days at home. Because she couldn't afford the time for medical treatment, she found a way out—substituting one stress for another. People who have traveled by train in Russia will understand when I say that that is a radical remedy!

Those who worked as my parents did—and there were many—were obviously thinking about their careers and promotions. But their main incentive was the desire to give something better to us, their children.

People also were concerned about their pensions. That's why they tried to work in the same place for a long time, setting a high value on the notes in their service-record books. To lose this document was worse than losing a passport. Without either of these documents, a person is nobody and nothing. A registration record is in the passport. If a person isn't registered, he or she will not be given employment. If a person has no employment, he or she will not be registered! Many people tried to solve this puzzle in one way or another. But anyone caught in such a situation was regarded with suspicion. Public opinion was cruel and intolerant: "Decent people don't find themselves in such situations. Decent people have a registration, a passport, and a job." Any deviation, even a half-step to one or the other side, met with disapproval. We Russians were used to marching in this regimented column formation.

The Fear of Getting Out of Line

I knew from personal experience the painful and humiliating consequences of stepping out of the column, even though it ended up being only a kind of flick on the nose. One November, when Julia was a baby, my husband, Sergei, and I decided to participate in the universal celebration of the Russian Revolution. We joined the parade that marched through the streets of Sverdlovsk, to end up in the main city square, taking Julia in her pram with us. But we soon fell out of step. It was unbearably cold, and not only were we getting chilled ourselves, but we had overestimated our little daughter's endurance. We decided to find a shorter route to the festival square, where loud music was playing and a voice kept shouting out cheerful words of greeting and salutation to all the marching columns.

When we reached the central square, we tried to join another column that was marching toward the monument to Lenin. But our attempt to join the column was suddenly stopped. Policemen, red-faced from the bitter cold, began frenziedly pushing us and the others who tried to join away from the marchers toward a side street. None of the marchers stopped and interceded for us—not even for me, a young woman with a baby. When the police got us into the side street, they gave vent to words. Swear words and filthy expletives I had never heard poured down on me. We looked frantically around, trying to find a way of escape, but the street was blocked at the other end by a Black Maria police van—something I had never seen before. All of us in the side street were being shoved toward the open doors of the van, where hands reached out to grab us. I began shouting too, trying to make excuses. Then I suddenly jerked at Julia's pram with all my strength, and somehow, miraculously, we slipped away.

That's how important it was not ever to leave the track, not even by chance and without any hidden purpose. That's how important it was to march in column formation, preferably as near the head of the column as possible.

But after perestroika, what did the country do for those who had never fallen out of step, who had worked harder and more diligently than others, who had all their papers in order? Nothing. Their pensions, as often as not, were less than those of people who had never worked at all or who had done poor quality work. Moral losses can cause more suffering than financial ones. Such poor pensioners had to suffer both morally and materially: they suffered from humiliation, and with almost no means they barely managed to survive.

The Need for Justice and Dignity

I soon came to understand another reason why we needed Methodism: Methodism can return to us the justice and the dignity that have been taken away from us. My grandfather was robbed of justice and dignity, along with his belongings, when he was forcefully evicted from his home, fearing for his children's lives, and had to learn to submit. For all Russians, the incipient dignity that our parents tried to foster in us at home was immediately trampled on from outside.

Our country did not like upstarts, infant prodigies or even champions; it distrusted the tall and handsome, the peculiar and original, the bright and witty. Everyone had to conform, to be part of the same "smiling-faced" family. Thus "step-children" appeared—those who didn't conform to the enforced "family" state of our large country. These were people who did not like uniformity of dress and ideas, who did not like to march in formation. And stepchildren are just stepchildren, aren't they? They're not blood relations. So they can be corralled without our feeling guilty. We need law and order.

Take, for instance, the principle "Ignorance of the law doesn't relieve you of responsibility." We had to live by this principle, no matter how absurd the application. The criminal code was published for official use and only lawyers could read it. But ordinary civilians had to answer for any infringement and be punished in full. People were intimidated and put in prison without having any idea that they had broken a law. Police and the KGB used this principle without any restrictions.

I had an experience with this principle during my second pregnancy. It was not an easy pregnancy, but I was bearing it with joyful elation: I was waiting for a son, dreaming of him, all the time seeing in my imagination, for some reason, a cute, red-haired little boy.

At the beginning of my eighth month, I got a phone call. "You have lost your passport and must come to the City Department of Internal Affairs," a law officer informed me peremptorily.

A mixture of guilt and foreboding struck me in the pit of my stomach, near the place where my baby sometimes unceremoniously gave me a kick. *How could I? Where? When?* I thought, terror-stricken, unable to think logically or to answer. But then my head cleared. "My passport is here, in this house," I answered, glad that the misunderstanding was over. "I have not lost it."

"You have lost your passport," repeated the policeman woodenly, "and it has been used by a dangerous criminal. You must come here immediately."

"But I have nobody to leave my young daughter with, and she is running a temperature."

It didn't matter. I had to go. My heart thumping madly, I tried to resist, not wanting to take my sick nine-year-old daughter across town to the Department of Internal Affairs. But I had no choice. I would have go there and prove that I had not done anything reprehensible. I was caught by the cunning hook of "law and order."

I caught a taxi, my thoughts jumping a hundred times faster than the second hand on the taxi clock. At the Internal Affairs office, I ran upstairs with Julia, opened the door of the official's room, and stood stock-still under the fixed stare of a slender young man.

"Leave the child in the corridor," he said.

"But she can't stay there without me. She'll be frightened and . . ."

"Leave the girl in the corridor," the officer interrupted.

"But . . ."

"I must interrogate you," he snapped, and he bent his head over the record of evidence that was lying on the table.

I was stunned. I hadn't expected this. I had thought I would just produce my passport and hear his apology for the mistake. Instead, the interrogation lasted four hours.

At first, I briskly produced my passport and explained that I had never lost it at all. The young man paid no attention. "Where and when did you lose your passport?" he asked. Again I tried to explain—to no avail. After hearing the question for the fifth or sixth time, I burst out crying.

I don't think I would ever have understood anything if the official had not begun shouting and yelling at me. Finally it hit me: *The rotter is shouting at me! Me, the woman with another life beating inside her. He is shouting at my son!* The mother in me rose in rebellion, and the shy and frightened little girl that I still was hid behind that mother's back.

"Stop shouting at me! How dare you!" I told the official, even striking the table with my palm. How I wanted to hit that mean wretch, but the table and my belly prevented me.

Suddenly I myself began asking questions. "Who used my passport? What did that man do? Why are you keeping me here? Why don't you listen to what I am saying? And why do you allow yourself to shout at me? Here is my passport! Why do you keep repeating the same question like a parrot?"

"Ah! You even insult me on top of everything!" screamed the interrogator. "I've got a witness here!"

Only then did I notice another man in the room. His face looked more normal to me, and I said to him, "You, at least, must see that it is all a mistake!"

The man dropped his eyes without answering.

Then, in a flash, I remembered. Four or five years before, I had picked up a new passport at the police station. When I got home, I had left it in my handbag, which I hung on the hall stand. That evening I went to the post office to pick up a small parcel. While standing in line, I got out my new passport and began to flip through it. *Horrors!* The passport was covered with my daughter's scrawls and scribbling. She had "filled in" the passport with the thorough calligraphy of a three-year-old! Julia had pulled a chair into the hall, under the handbag, climbed up on the chair, and pulled out the passport. After filling it in with "fine letters," she put it back into my handbag. The situation brought me a lot of trouble at the time, first with the unreceived parcel, and then with a special commission, where I had to answer a lot of questions and pay a fine before receiving a new passport.

"I've remembered!" I cried out joyfully to the two men in the office, and I told them this story. Again I expected to hear an apology. But it seemed that I had only poured oil on the flame.

"You see, you were trying to conceal such a fact from justice." The interrogator shook his head reproachfully and began to stare hard at me, as if trying to see something new. "And thou art not such a naïve girl as thou seemest before." (His use of thee and thou, the familiar second-person singular, was a method of condescension. That tactic was the final blow.)

Now the interrogation took another turn. "What didst thou do with that spoiled passport?"

I don't remember. I don't remember what I did with it. I was talking to myself, trying to jog my memory. *Did I throw it out? No, I couldn't have. Is it at home? No, it can't be!*

Then suddenly I was on the offensive again. "Why are you pretending?" I said firmly. "There is an order in our country: the spoiled passports are left at the police station. So it is lying somewhere here, and you know it!"

Here my heart missed a beat. *They know everything without my telling them. They are just jeering at me. I don't understand what is happening—something impossible, absurd. It's not happening to me. Is it a bad dream? But my daughter has been sitting in the corridor for three hours.*

No, it was no dream. It was the horror and gloom which, as I came to know later, hundreds of thousands went through during the years of the Soviet power. When, hypnotized by the gravity of the accusations they were charged with and by the interrogators' attitude, they pleaded guilty to political and criminal offenses they hadn't committed, they were imprisoned for ten, fifteen, twenty-five years—or they were shot.

But I did not know about all that as yet. I still believed that "my militia is guarding me," as the popular song of the times put it—a phrase that acquired a malicious meaning in later years.

The interrogation continued. Now I was asked short questions.

"Where do your parents work? Where do they live? When did they move into the new flat? How are they doing the repair work? Where did they get the money for buying the paint, the wallpaper, the sink, the toilet bowl? Where did they buy them?"

I was dumbfounded. *How could they know that my parents were doing repair work in their apartment? Why should anyone care about it anyway? What has it got to do with my passport?*

After more of this absurdity, I found myself in another, equally absurd situation.

"I shall tell you a secret." The interrogator addressed me in a friendly manner now, using the polite "you" and even trying to smile playfully. "If you'll help us with the information against your mother, we shall forget the story with your lost passport."

Oh God! Hasn't he understood that I did not lose my passport?

The interrogator's pen was busily scratching against the paper. I could see the file swelling: new pages were being added one after another.

"So what can you tell us about the repair work in your parents' flat?"

"I don't understand! What has the repair work got to do with all this? My father bought all the building materials in Moscow and sent them here in a container after he finished his study at the USSR Academy of Sciences. You must know that it is impossible to buy anything in Sverdlovsk."

And then, like a bolt from the blue, came the truth.

"We've got an anonymous letter here, saying that your mother has stolen all the building materials from her place of work." The interrogator offered me an unsigned letter, written in an unfamiliar hand.

"It isn't true!" I groaned, throwing aside the dirty sheet with disgust.

"How will you prove it?" asked the interrogator spitefully.

How, indeed? Who will believe me? Then I suddenly had a mental picture of our family's teasing Father because he kept every piece of paper that came to the house, even quite useless ones. He always carefully stored all his checks and receipts. "Just in case," he would say. "It may come in handy."

"You had only to ask my father about the building materials, and he would have satisfied your interest." I was quite calm now, feeling the interrogation coming to an end.

"Sign your testimony, then," the interrogator said with an unexpected sweetness.

My testimony? But I was ready to sign anything just to get out of that room. I began to read, absentmindedly at first, until I was stopped by words I had never uttered. I began to reread the text. It was a condemnation of me and my parents.

"For shame! I never said this! Rewrite it!"

"I've got a witness who will confirm that I am right," the interrogator threatened.

Only after I began to repeat, word for word, what I had said during our four-hour "talk," did the interrogator, amazed by my photographic memory, or maybe afraid of something, give up.

"Dictate what you said, only sign it." I dictated and I signed—not knowing that, by law, I didn't have to sign anything, that I could not be interrogated without an advocate! I knew nothing. But God helped me. And God saved us all from disgrace. It was a miracle that all the documents concerning the building materials my parents had been buying for three years were kept intact.

Only when I got home, and with my parents' assistance, did I discover what my tormentor might have done to me. Even so, I found it hard to believe. So I went to the regional public procurator, who put an end to all the nightmare around our family and apologized to us officially. It turned out that the root of the matter was my mother's job. Mother had been working for twenty years as an administrator at the Medical Institute, a teaching institution. Before entrance examinations, all the young people who were eager to enter the institute came to Mother's office with their documents. Once, a girl with forged documents and influential relatives in both the local government and the KGB came to the office. Mother refused to take the girl's documents and, as a result, made a lot of influential and vindictive enemies who tried from then on to humiliate and intimidate her in every possible way—including the anonymous letter. We eventually discovered that the letter was written by a woman who'd been my friend since we were fourteen. All those years I'd been helping her, trying to lift her out of the swamp of ignorance and dullness she and her parents lived in.

An anonymous letter in itself is of no importance. It's just a piece of paper. But in our country this Piece of Paper can have a monstrous destroying force. As a result of one, my son was born prematurely, a month before his time.

The Need to Confront the Pain of the Past

Why am I writing all this? Some people may find it a strange way of telling about Russian Methodists. Some, perhaps, will not see my point. But it is very important for me to be open with my readers and with myself, so that everyone reading this can feel the tragedies, the pain, the forces that brought formerly unbelieving people to the Methodist Church.

So many people in Russia have been hurt and humiliated unjustly. Many died without being rehabilitated. Many are still keeping family secrets, afraid of sharing them, though everything is long forgotten. One day the KGB archives in Sverdlovsk were opened, and the horrified town learned that just near the town gates there was a nameless burial ground. Thousands of guiltless people had been secretly shot, the dead and those left for dead pushed into ditches and covered with earth. Relatives who had been patiently looking for their fathers, mothers, brothers, or sisters lost in prisons, went hopefully to this place. Thus a new "cemetery" was born. People began to affix the photos and names of their relatives to the trunks of the trees that had grown in the area.

When my father took me there, I was shaken by the spirit of violence and sadness I felt hovering over the burial ground. I stopped at a little tablet with the same family name written four times on it—Schegolev. A father and three sons had been killed. At the time, it seemed just a chance moment, a chance stop. But it wasn't! A year later one of my parishioners, a prematurely old woman, came up to me.

"I want to tell you my secret," she said, and she told me her unbearably sad story. She was a Schegolev, the daughter and sister of those four men. As the relative of "enemies of the people," she had been afraid to marry and have children, lest she should thus condemn them to undeserved pain and humiliation!

How many more such people are there among my parishioners? I wondered—children of murdered Orthodox priests, dispossessed peasants, political and economic "criminals." For seventy years the country had been flying towards the "bright Communist future," but on the way riding roughshod over the best and the most honest. Yet even in prison camps, prisoners sang about our large country, its fields, forests, and rivers, and of how free they felt in it!

When guests from America came to Sverdlovsk in 1991 to celebrate the first anniversary of our church and to take part in the ceremony of blessing the land on which we would build our church, they were astonished, even staggered, by the hospitality and cordiality of our Methodists, by their trust and sincerity. They expected Soviet people to be quite different, perhaps antagonistic or suspicious. They were also surprised by the difference between us and Moscow citizens; they saw fewer sad-faced people here in Sverdlovsk and heard no complaints or lamentations. What is more, our parishioners as often as not seemed to be better dressed than our overseas friends! The fact is that our tactful guests had purposely dressed very modestly lest they should embarrass us. As for us, suspecting nothing, we had dressed for the occasion, putting on our best clothes. We couldn't afford to look pitiful, nor did we want anyone to know that some of us had no apartments, others couldn't find work, and some were going hungry.

That characteristic puzzled Bishop Oden's wife, Marilyn. She also couldn't understand why our parishioners did not respond when she asked them to share their life stories with her. She wanted to write a book about Russian Christians. Only a few people complied with her wish, and only after I had asked them several times.

One day an older parishioner exclaimed, "But can't you see? It is so painful!" After that I stopped asking. Yes, the path to faith for all of us was very long and painful. And, I confess, I couldn't bring myself to sit down and write out my story for Marilyn either. What was so difficult? Like most of my parishioners, I was unable to bear the pain of re-experiencing all the horrors of the past. Our wounds were still bleeding. In order to be understood, one must tell everything, and that is painful. And that was what I wrote in my apology to our new friend in Louisiana, who really wanted "to understand the Russian soul."

5.

LEARNING TO BE A PASTOR

Blessing and Suffering

Now that I was the leader of our parishioners, one question kept torturing me: "What do I have to give these long-suffering and work-worn people?" As a girl, I was sheltered by my parents. I married early and had spent all my life beside my children. I had never traveled by myself or been beyond the borders of my country. I did not really know people and I was naïve and trusting.

Early in the summer of 1991, not long before the first anniversary of our church, Dwight Ramsey unexpectedly invited my father and me to Shreveport. The idea seemed incredible, for we had none of the things necessary for a trip abroad: an international passport, a visa, or plane tickets. We could get international passports only in Moscow, at the Ministry of Foreign Affairs. So that's where I went.

I want to describe a curious incident in connection with this impregnable institution. Only an improvident person would have gone to the Ministry of Foreign Affairs without any kind of backing or patronage, as I did, and certainly not without a gift. When I got there, the employees kept sending me from one room to another. The process might have lasted forever, I think, had I not lost patience! I found the chief's office, opened the door, and walked in. At first I thought there were two men sitting behind the table, so powerful and huge did the chief appear. His face was swollen and puffy, and I could hardly discern his tiny eyes, which looked at me attentively.

"Well, what can I do for you?" he drawled lazily.

Acting on impulse, I opened my handbag, got out my Bible, and said, "This is for you."

"Who are you?" he asked, suddenly bending toward me so that his body almost lay across the table strewn with hundreds of applications.

"I am from the Methodist Church," I whispered timidly, not knowing what I was expected to answer.

"Give me your documents," he said. Then, almost as in a fairy tale, I was led to different rooms for one procedure after another, until finally I was given the proper papers for the passports and visas. That meant we practically had them. Now all we had to get were the airline tickets. All the savings I had—about 2,250 rubles (equal to around $700 then)—would barely cover the cost of a one-way ticket. Besides that, I had to have money to pay my huge long-distance phone bill, and I would need some money for souvenirs and gifts.

As it turned out, Dwight had already purchased our tickets for us. We learned the details only after we got to Shreveport. After he had bought our tickets, Dwight realized that it wasn't a simple matter to send them to us. If he declared the amount he paid for them, he would have to pay an exorbitant amount for insurance. What should he do? He decided to pay $48 to send them by express mail to Moscow, knowing that we do not have express mail in Sverdlovsk—and he did a lot of praying. He had been praying for four days before I telephoned from Moscow just to say that we had the visas and the tickets were in our pockets. I had no idea what a storm was raging in his soul while I stood in line for six hours at the Moscow Central Telegraph Office in order to phone him. If I had known the state he was in, I would have gladly stood in line for ten hours!

My father and I had fourteen unforgettable days in Shreveport with the people of Broadmoor United Methodist Church. I felt as if locks had been opened in my heart: I trusted everyone and everyone trusted me. I was immersed in a sea of love, goodwill, elation, and delight! It is impossible to tell about Methodists from Russia without telling about the Methodists from Broadmoor, because the Broadmoor congregation taught me what I needed to learn: lessons of faith, sincerity of prayer, the joy of fellowship. Members of this congregation nurtured and supported me: Rosie and Jim Wood, who became my family; Gay Ramsey and her children, Jinny, Kim, and David, who were always looking after my father and me; Gaye and Cal Cranor; Mary and Jim Waddle; Maureen and Carson Turnage; Paul Merkle; Brenda and Bob Haley; Pete and James Gillespie; Jason Weymar; Larry Hiller—and so many others.

How difficult it was to leave, but not because life in the United States is brighter and fuller. Actually, I wasn't surprised by the American way of life, even though this was my first trip abroad. No, it was difficult to leave because I was charmed by the people and didn't want to part from them. I was still so weak as a Christian, so unprepared as a pastor. I not only needed all my new friends' prayers, but I needed their presence as well. We had been able to understand one another even though my English was very rough. But I hadn't needed an interpreter—people understood me and I understood them. We were speaking the language of the heart.

At home, tragedy was waiting for me. Five-year-old Paul had pneumonia! Paul was already ill before I left for the States. When I telephoned my family, they didn't say that Paul's condition was serious. Paul had not fully recovered when my husband took the children to Sochi, on the Black Sea, for a holiday. The change of climate affected Paul, and he developed pneumonia.

When I arrived in Sochi, I refused to acknowledge Paul's serious condition. Usually I was intuitively aware of my children's symptoms and was able to diagnose and treat them correctly. But now I lost my head and tried to deceive myself, not wanting to admit that Paul's life was in danger. After two weeks of joy and happiness in America, I couldn't believe that something frightful and unfair was happening. *Such things just cannot be! My little boy will be up and running around in no time,* I told myself. The morning I arrived, Paul said he wanted to be with people, so we decided to go for a walk. But he didn't have the strength to walk very far, so we sat down on a bench. When my husband and I tried to take Paul back to the room, he cried out pitifully, "I want to be with people!" Yet his facial expression betrayed his weariness.

The doctor came by that evening. As she was taking Paul's pulse, he lost consciousness. The doctor said Paul was suffering from a bad case of respiratory and cardiac deficiency and would have to be taken to the hospital.

At the hospital, the doctor tried to send me away from the ward, saying, "You are not supposed to be here!"

"Do you want to find a demented woman among the bushes in the morning?" I responded. The doctor relented and allowed me to stay with Paul—for five days in the intensive care ward, then twenty days in a regular ward. I had no sleeping space, nor was I fed, because I was in the hospital against regulations. But I would not leave. Sometimes Paul lost consciousness and cried out in delirium. For much of the time I read the Bible aloud to him. I read because I was unable to do anything else, except pray. I prayed aloud and people in the hospital thought I had gone off my head. I stopped only when it was necessary to scrub the pots and tidy up the ward. Then I resumed reading again. When Paul fell asleep I went on reading and kept asking myself, "Why is this happening?" Then I read that "the Lord disciplines those whom he loves" (Heb. 12:6). *So the Lord loves me,* I thought. Then I knew that he would not leave us in this trial.

"Paul, aren't you tired of listening to me read the Bible?" I asked once, when he was lying quietly. "Shall I read some fairy tales to you?"

"All right," he responded listlessly. But I had hardly read a couple of pages when he said urgently, "Mummy, it's better to read the Bible! I'm tired." It was the first time he had asked for anything after four frightful days.

After that the doctors were surprised by the sudden changes in Paul's condition. One day he sat up, then took a few steps, though just two days before he hadn't even been able to hold up his head, it hurt so much. Not only his lungs but the whole of his tiny body was affected.

"This is a miracle," the doctors said when we asked to be discharged from the hospital. We were desperate to leave that terrible place. Every morning small corpses covered with sheets were taken out of the wards. There was no medicine! My parents had sent us the necessary medicine by plane, asking people to pass it on to us. Those people found us in the hospital, but by then Paul was already on the way to recovery.

Sergei spent his days and nights near the hospital, while he looked after Julia—our darling fourteen-year-old, who had to grow up so early.

Through Paul's illness I came to know and believe that prayers can heal. Much later, our parishioner Tatiana Zhdanova, an excellent cardiologist, said to me, "How shameful that there's no medicine in the hospital, while people look at me so hopefully. Then I have only one method left—to treat them by prayer." I understood her perfectly.

We were discharged from the hospital only after we signed a document saying that we would not raise any claim in case Paul's condition took a turn for the worse during the plane flight home. An ambulance took us straight to the plane, and the doctor was with us until the takeoff. Fearing Paul might develop lung edema, I monitored his breathing during the flight. But another miracle: the longer the flight lasted, the merrier my son became. *He's alive!* I remember thinking. *Soon we'll be home!*

When we got home, the first thing Paul wanted to do was to light a candle. I was ready to do anything he wanted. He looked at the flame for a long time. Suddenly he said, "Mummy, I know what God is like. I have just seen a church with a dome and metal letters on the church: METHODIST CHURCH!"

I took this as another of God's signs to me. In the hospital, I had mentally vowed that I would stay at home with my son and take care of him. But again I understood: *Methodism is my vocation. I can't get away from it.*

Later, Paul revealed another of his gifts. Out of the blue he asked me, "Mummy, what do you think about Victor?" referring to my friend from my school days, and one of the first among us to meet Dwight. The fact that Paul had used the first name of an adult was strange. "Do you think he is a believer?" he went on. "No, he is very far from God. Look—" and he moved his index fingers far away from each other. "Victor is far from you, so he is far from God, too."

Somewhat puzzled, I asked him about each of the first members of our Methodist association. He told me what their relationship with God was. Had I known at the time that it was no game . . .

Ordained by the Light

After a long interruption—the nearly two months of my absence—our regular meetings began again, this time in the building of the Medical Institute. Because of our presence, my mother was to have problems later on. But now we met with general delight and enthusiasm. We wanted to be together, and we felt united—"old-timers" and neophytes.

My parishioners gave me so much. Every sermon, every personal talk gave me a chance to learn something from them. These people were fed up with mere words. They needed *the* Word. Distrustful, spiritually bankrupt, disappointed, embittered—they all needed something different.

But not my words, however beautiful and honest, emotional and heartfelt. The congregation needed God's word. Where could I find it?

I am not a prophet, not a priest, not a theologian. I'm just some sort of hybrid: a local pastor, but without a thorough knowledge of the Bible, without any special education; an electrochemical engineer behind the pulpit. How can I convey God's message to these people?

Once, after spending a week preparing my sermon, I fell on my knees in despair, feeling that whatever I said in my sermon, it would just be more "information" for my parishioners. I asked the Lord to speak through me. "O Lord," I prayed, "I give myself to Thee. Use my lips, my voice, and my heart. Fill my vessel with Thy life-giving force! Speak through me. Act through me. Bless me, Lord, for serving Thee and people. Amen."

A torrent of light and gladness came down on me, and I rose to my feet, full of strength and confidence. That day, as soon as I began my sermon, a miracle happened. I opened my mouth to give the sermon I had prepared—but, no, I couldn't! My lips pronounced quite different words. It was not *my* voice that I heard. Everyone present was sitting so quietly that I felt uneasy, but I went on talking. I spoke to the point, smoothly and calmly, not too emotionally. But the tears were running down my cheeks. My parishioners were in tears, too. God Himself was speaking to us.

God blessed me and helped me on my way to becoming a pastor by sending good people to me. First Dwight, then all my friends from Broadmoor, then more and more people from different towns and churches in Louisiana, Mississippi, Tennessee, Oklahoma, Missouri, Kansas, Florida, and Texas—pastors and members who prayed for Russia, for our parishioners, for my family and myself. I know how much these prayers have helped.

The Threat of Revolution

A few years earlier we had been shocked by news of the military coup in Chile. But in August 1991, a coup d'etat was happening right here in our country, before our eyes, in the presence of those who had been building and defending this now-departing social system. It's difficult to describe the feelings of all of us who watched. I certainly can't pin them down with one word. Some were glad that perestroika, the restructuring of the nation, might be stopped; others deplored the possibility. But it was a universal shock, generating feelings of both apathy and fear.

I spent the whole day of August 19 near my telephone, trying to get information from my friends in Moscow. Television and radio reported nothing. But when the ballet *Swan Lake* was broadcast on TV, we understood that things were in a bad way. We knew from experience that if symphony concerts or ballets were broadcast on all state TV programs, it meant that someone had died or there had been a change of leadership! As was our custom, we could only wait for the official information. At first we had nothing but conjectures, then there were rumors about a coup and Gorbachev's arrest. Even our parents, with all the surprises of their lives, had not seen the like.

My members telephoned me: "Lydochka!" they said. "We are so lucky to have our church. Together we shall hold out! It is not so terrible together!"

Other parishioners phoned me and tried to cheer me up: "We are together!" It was extraordinary: we were not afraid! We just shared new information. For the first time I began to feel that my flat was not unlike a headquarters. People kept phoning and coming to the apartment. Only one member got frightened. "Lydia!" she said. "Are you alone? I must talk to you confidentially. Where do you keep the lists of all parishioners? Hide them in some safe place or still better, destroy them!"

One of our members happened to be in Moscow at the must crucial point. She had been near the white house and with her bare hands had torn cobbles out of the pavement to use as weapons. She hadn't slept for two nights. When she returned to Sverdlovsk, she showed me her hands as a great secret. (This young, beautiful woman did not become a Methodist in the long run. She was constantly harassed by doubts as to whether she, a Moslem woman, might attend a Christian church. She liked attending our services and helped us for a while in our school. But eventually she left us to pursue her business interests.)

An Official Dedication and Consecration

We did not know then that members of our sister church in Louisiana, who were getting ready for their first visit to us, had conducted a special service for Russia and for us Russian Methodists during these crisis days. As for us, these events had united us. Apparently Soviet people really need "a great misfortune" to forget about their troubles, offenses, lack of money, and ill health, and to make them unite for a common cause. We were grateful that our unknown friends from Shreveport were not afraid to visit us in September, just after the attempted coup.

But it seemed that God went on testing us. The plane from Moscow with the long-awaited guests could not take off on time because of fog. But we were already at the Koltsovo airport, forty minutes by car from Ekaterinburg, dressed in our best and carrying flowers, before we learned of the delay. We eagerly awaited every announcement and didn't think of returning home. To go home and try to phone to Koltsovo is hopeless for at least two reasons. First, not everyone has a phone at home, and public phones are practically always out of order. Second, even if phone access is available it's hard to get through because the airport line is almost always busy. Furthermore, only two or three families in our church have cars, so if we had gone home, there was no guarantee that we could get a ride back to the airport in time to meet the flight.

So we did the most reliable thing—we stayed at the airport. We didn't want to miss the moment of meeting our guests. We waited for twenty-four hours! Just before sunrise, lying curled up on hard benches, we began to giggle nervously—*what if there are fleas here?* We were sure we could feel the fleas biting. All that time our American friends, unwashed and uncomfortable, were trying to while away the hours in the crowded intourist terminal of the domestic airport Domodedovo, just south of Moscow. That was the way we met the next morning: sleepy, crumpled, hungry, but infinitely happy.

We got our guests into the cars as quickly as we could and drove toward Sverdlovsk at top speed, because the ceremony of dedicating the land for the church was already scheduled to begin. Several hundred people were waiting for us in Methodist Park, the name we had given to the twenty acres of land we had been allowed for building the church. We didn't have to tell our visitors when we arrived at our destination; they could hear the singing of Methodist hymns, amplified by loudspeakers. As we drove up, the crowd surged forward spontaneously to meet us. Only when the boys' choir, conducted by Yuri Bondar, began singing our favorite hymn, "What a Friend We Have in Jesus," did silence fall, and we could feel peace filling every cell of our bodies. The forgotten sensation of serenity and safety we used to have in childhood now came back to us. We were standing there together, children of one Father. Faith, hope, and love were born in us on that land.

The service began with a blessing by the bishop of Northern Europe, Hans Växby. We sang more hymns and prayed. Then Bishop William Oden conducted the special service for consecrating the land, with Lena Stepanova as the interpreter. As part of the liturgy, Bishop Oden spoke three long phrases, from which I caught only a few words. Lena translated them into three short sentences. All of us, directed by the bishop, took bunches of grass, raised them high, and repeated after Lena in Russian:

"We are blessing this land.

"We are blessing this land.

"We are blessing this land."*

At that point a suspicion crept into my mind: *Do we have the right to bless the land ourselves?* But I drove that thought away. Later on, though, I was distressed when that doubt was brought up by others. Women in kerchiefs, believers from other churches who had come to the ceremony, approached me one after another saying, "People have no right to bless. Only God can do it." I felt awkward about asking any of our guests about the problem, feeling they would think the question showed rank ignorance on my part. And after the ceremony was over, I forgot about it. It wasn't until much later that I found the answer to my questions in *The Book of Worship*—we had been dedicating the land to God.

That evening we had a real public worship service in the very plain hall of the Sverdlovsk Philharmonic Theater. The organ played and the boys' choir sang again, their pure voices rising up to the high vault of the hall. There were no vacant seats. Public worship services were held on two days, September 21 and 22, 1991. The first one lasted three

---

* Bishop Oden quoted from *The Book of Worship,* as follows:
    To the glory of God the Father, who has called us by his grace;
    To the honor of his Son, who loved us and gave himself for us;
    To the praise of the Holy Spirit, who illumines and sanctifies us;
      We dedicate this land.
  For the worship of God in prayer and praise;
  For the preaching of the everlasting Gospel;
  For the celebration of the holy Sacraments;
      We dedicate this land.
  In gratitude for the labors of all who love and serve this church;
  In loving remembrance of those who have finished their course;
  In the hope of a blessed immortality through Jesus Christ our Lord,
      We dedicate this land.

hours, because there was a long line of people who wanted to be baptized. We decided to baptize children first. '

Both Bishop Växby and Dwight preached. Among other things, Dwight talked of his love for Sverdlovsk and its people. After he sat down, he was unable to restrain his tears, and people in the hall cried as well. I was sitting behind Dwight with Spurgeon Dunnam, and I heard Dwight say, "When I die, I want my body to be buried in my beloved town Shreveport. But I'd like my heart to be separated from my body and buried in Sverdlovsk, the town where my heart is living now."

I felt so thankful to Dwight for his love of us, for his loyalty, that I vowed to be faithful to Dwight, whatever happened, as he was faithful to us. I was not the only one staggered by his words. That evening 132 people were baptized. And three years later I listened to a sermon from Olga Kotsuba, my associate pastor, in which, still shaken, she told us what a revelation his words were.

That was the day I became a pastor. I knelt and made a vow before God and people to serve them faithfully. Then I was given the right to baptize and to serve the Eucharist, that sacred rite.

Reaching Out to Prisoners

Some time after my consecration, Yelena Tischenko, one of our parishioners, came to me with a proposal that I hold a service for prisoners in one of the Sverdlovsk prisons. Yelena's husband, Vasili, worked at the Administration of Reformatory Institutions, and this idea, naturally, was born in their family. I couldn't say no. (Much later I learned that that was one of my negative traits—not knowing how to say no.) But having said yes, I had to figure out how to accomplish the task.

It wouldn't be an easy task for me. Since childhood I had hated all criminals. I hated them pathologically, thinking that all of them should be shot. Now I had to go to them and say, "God loves you."

Loves them for what? I kept asking myself, getting ready for this service. Then I remembered my surreal experience of being interrogated, and I thought, *What if some of these prisoners had been convicted wrongly? I must help them.* I didn't tell anyone about my doubts. And having found for myself a positive motivation for visiting a prison camp, I ventured to go there with my sermon.

But when I stood in front of four hundred close-cropped, black-jacketed men, I was panic-stricken. *My God! Where am I?* I was standing high on a stage, and eight hundred eyes were fastened on me rapaciously. The men had not seen a woman for five to ten years. My naïveté had let me down again. I knew that only violators and murderers were sitting in the hall. And the numbers were growing as more prisoners came in. No vacant seats were left, and men were standing in the aisles. The picture was becoming more and more dismal. Suddenly I felt like seizing the hem of my black dress and stretching it down to the floor, so unbearable was it to feel those hungry, almost brutal, eyes on me. *I need a robe to wrap myself in from head to foot!* I thought in despair.

That first moment, when I was trying to collect my thoughts in front of the prisoners, seemed to last as long as a year. They say that before people die, they see all the events of their life rushing through their minds. Something like that happened to me then. And I thought of Granddad lying silently with his face to the wall, reliving his life in his memory, especially the bird-cherry trees.

Memory! That was the thing I must talk about to these men. God enabled me to talk with them—the embittered, the brutal, the convicts who hated all the world—to talk unemotionally, without any pretty words as though I were using their manner of speaking. I spoke of the memories of the heart: childhood, happy or otherwise; grandparents, mother and father, brothers and sisters; the women they loved, faithful or faithless; their hometowns or villages. Little by little the atmosphere of the hall became peaceful and calm. I felt the thick, cold wall of distrust between the prisoners and myself disappear, along with my desire to wrap myself in something large and long. Those eyes that had looked at me with a wolflike glitter at first, then (after I was introduced as a pastor of some church no one had ever heard of) with a sarcastic cast, now became more human and warm. In that black, swaying crowd, full of malicious buzzing at first, then turned silent, I could now discern individual faces. They were people sitting in front of me now.

I went on talking: about those who waited for them at home; about their relatives having to wait in long lines in shops, being without work, sometimes without money; about how their relatives were counting the days till they were reunited with them, and meanwhile were sending everything they could here, to this "zone."

Then I noticed a gray head bending lower and lower. Was the man dropping off to sleep? But his hands suddenly shot up to his face and his shoulders shuddered with childlike helpless and unalleviated weeping.

After the sermon, more than 170 people wanted to be baptized.

"May I baptize prisoners?" I asked Dwight when I phoned him after the meeting. I was afraid I'd done something wrong. When he laughed happily, I knew his answer.

Over the next year, 172 prisoners in this particular prison were baptized by Dwight and me, assisted by other visiting ministers. I can't say which of them I baptized by myself or how many we baptized together. In any case, we are just instruments in the hands of the Most High, and all of the prisoners were baptized by our Lord.

During those sacred ceremonies there were both lofty and earthly moments. Once it seemed to me that I had already baptized the man who stood in front of me. When I hesitated, the man repeated frantically, "I haven't been baptized. I haven't been baptized." I placed my hand on his head and realized that I had already baptized him—his head was wet! What he needed, I realized, was just one thing: someone to touch his close-cropped head again.

Probably many crimes are committed by people who saw very little kindness in their lives. So from hatred I went to the other extreme—I felt compassion for every one of the prisoners.

I shall never forget one day, when about thirty men came onto the stage during the service to be baptized. Usually when I baptize, I see and hear nothing besides the person in front of me and the words I am saying. But this day I suddenly felt light—bright light—coming from the direction of the altar, but I couldn't raise my head while saying the prayers. When at last I did look, I saw a fire on the altar. The candlestick that we had been using for a year had caught fire, and the flame was so large it seemed that the table itself was burning. It was very difficult to put the fire out. That was the moment when the Lord sent us all a sign: "I am here," He seemed to be saying. "Accept Me and sin no more. You are healed by Me."

Limited Resources

I discovered that trying to visit prisoners more than two times a month was physically demanding. After each visit I was exhausted. While I was there I gave them everything. I left pale, dead tired, and feeling a frightening emptiness in my heart. A Christian psychologist once saw me while I was baptizing during our own church service. "You don't spare your strength," she told me. "You exhaust yourself. You don't know how to defend yourself." Her ruthless diagnosis: "You'll not be able to last even two years. So you must build a wall between the parishioners and yourself."

Surprised, I answered, "That is impossible! How can I baptize through a wall? How can I love through a wall?" But then I felt hurt that no one had taught me how to protect myself from emotional exhaustion.

With every man I baptized at the prison I, too, died to sin and rose from the dead with Christ. Otherwise, the rite would be a lie on my part. So every baptism in prison took all my strength. Afterwards, my strength would be wonderfully restored, but the short interval between exhaustion and restoration was excruciating.

Behind the scenes at the prison, I tried to find a pianist who could play during the service. "No problem," said one of the officers. "We'll invite a prisoner to play."

I didn't know then that prisoners responded to "requests" very quickly in that model prison; they were afraid if they did not comply that they would be transferred to a prison colony where conditions would be, to put it mildly, unspeakable. So I didn't have to wait long before a tall, lean, sullen-faced man who walked with a limp came up to me. "You're Protestant," he snapped scornfully. "I'm an Orthodox believer! I'll not play!" But after the sermon that day he came up to me again and said, "I will play for you."

Vladimir Polukhin had spent eight years in prison gulags and in more moderate "prison zones."* I didn't ask him what he was imprisoned for, but I discerned the tragedy of his life after reading his poetry. Some time later he presented me with a book of his verses. Then I learned how tenderly he loved his mother, who was prematurely old and brokenhearted. In his conversations about life in Russia, he was both wise and cynical, and sarcastic on the topic of politicians.

---

* Perhaps the closest equivalent to a "zone" is a minimum security prison in the U.S. *Ed.*

At the beginning of our acquaintance, Vladimir disconcerted me by asking, "Are you sure you are not in prison? You see, we both look at each other through the prison bars. I am on this side and you are on that side. Which of us is in prison? At least we prisoners are fed regularly and have work. There are no lines. And we are not afraid of taking a walk after dark here. But what about you, the 'free' people?"

That's true, I mentally agreed, and I thought about his observation for a long time. Our imprisonment had lasted for several generations. And things were still just as rotten now as they had been.

When I fell to thinking about the way my family and I were living, I was horrified. Standing in lines—a constant fact of life—was torture for me. I'd had my fill of it in childhood and had hated it ever since. I felt humiliated when looking at overfed shop assistants' faces, full of contempt for us customers. As for getting foodstuffs through pull and graft, I thought that humiliating, too.

Our refrigerator was always empty. The children met me in the evening, their faces pale, their eyes ringed with blue—but I arrived empty-handed. Occasionally, my parents and sister came to our rescue, buying butter or a chicken. In order to "save" Paul from the state kindergarten, my husband, Sergei, worked night shifts. During the day he looked after our son and also contrived to cook dinner, using whatever foodstuffs "God sent us." (That's an idiom commonly used in Russia!) Every morning he went to the nearest milk shop, but as often as not, after standing for two or three hours in the long line, he came back empty-handed.

More and more parishioners joined us, looking upon our church as their home. And they tried to do something for their church and for other parishioners. But some of the lessons we have to learn are not easy. Perhaps the most difficult for all of us has been the offering.

I personally found it impossible to conduct services and collect money. From the beginning, I kept postponing the taking of an offering. Even after we began to have regular worship services, I avoided that moment. Dwight grumbled. "You must do it. It's necessary," he insisted. Time and time again he repeated that by not having an offering we omitted an important lesson of Christianity—that "it is more blessed to give than to receive" (Acts 20:35). But my scruples prevented me from collecting money after speaking sacred words about God and praying. Money and worship seemed to me incompatible. And, worse, some people might even think that the money would be used to pay my salary.

It was actually a good thing that for the first year I didn't get any salary. It helped me feel independent. Independence—that's what I always strive for. Our community did periodically collect money for church needs. But times were hard, and we couldn't call on the members often. During the hard times my own family rescued me again. Otherwise, I'd have lost my telephone. It was disconnected periodically because I failed to pay for it regularly. And the telephone had become a lifeline for me: it connected me with the whole Methodist world. The telephone and then the fax became my manual, my seminary.

Helpers Join Me

My husband, Sergei, had undergone a stunning metamorphosis during this time. He is analytical by nature. A technically minded man, he had no mysticism in him. But while he was helping me more and more, unexpectedly he had become a believer himself, without really noticing when and how it had happened. Neither had I noticed this transitional moment. I was astonished one day when I saw him praying together with us, whereas formerly he used to stand aloof. Now there is no man more loyal and patient, modest and unpretentious beside me.

Sergei became my best friend and brother, shouldering all the unseen, but back-breaking burdens of our life. Even when he had gone without sleep for two or three nights in succession, on Sunday morning, tired and ashen-faced, he would take his technical equipment and reel of telephone wire, stuff his mike into the bag, and hurry to the church as early as possible in order to install the amplifying equipment and to check up on everything.

"Why on earth do you torture yourself?" I reproached him once, particularly in light of his grave chronic disease, the result of a nuclear waste explosion near Chelyabinsk,* about 150 miles south of Sverdlovsk, not far from where he had lived as a boy. His parents had died from cancer. Of all of us, he needed sleep, rest, and good food the most. "Why don't we hire a professional to handle the equipment?"

"You must not waste money!" he snapped.

It was no use arguing with him, but feeling proud of him makes me stronger.

Another miracle was the change that occurred in my father, Paul. It seemed only yesterday that he had tried to convert Dwight into an atheist. Father's attitude toward religion progressed from the level of "Well, at it again! Dwight this, Dwight that! He will never return!" to fervent praying for me when I failed to come home after work one day and nobody knew what had happened. When I returned at last, at midnight, Mother whispered in confusion, "Father looks awful. He's been fretting and dashing about the apartment. And then he began to pray."

It was not easy for him, in front of all his university professor friends, to change his convictions and to become

---

*The explosion of plutonium waste occurred in 1957 at a nuclear weapons plant, contaminating hundreds of square miles with strontium 90. Hundreds of people were killed and thousands were made ill. *Ed.*

a believer. Not only was he consumed with doubts, but he also suffered conflicting emotions. There was shocked disappointment with everything he had believed in, accompanied by the natural desire to find a new support. There was anxiety over me and my children, his grandchildren. And there was joy because all of us were working for a common cause. For a long time, out of confusion and embarrassment, he chose a seat for the church services as far as possible from the center of the hall, so that he could sit by himself.

His first decisive step was made the day I came home sobbing and told him how I had been humiliated by the university vice-president, a rude, heavy-set boor. I had never been treated like that except by other children when I was small. In charge of developing international contacts for the university, the vice-president begrudged my excessive (in his opinion) activity in the international sphere and zealously watched our "unexplainable" progress. There may have been other reasons, but I don't really know. When I was trying to get the necessary information on how to draw up an official invitation for the visit of the group from Shreveport, he grabbed me by the lapels of my coat and pushed me out of his office, yelling rude language at me.

There was no use in my making a complaint based on my feelings. Feelings are just feelings, of no interest to anyone! Yet even though the quality of our politicians and leaders can't be called superior, who could foresee such meanness? Nor could we expect any redress or protection. We were programmed to just "take" it. That's why I was so staggered at my father's reaction. He dropped out of the Communist Party and returned his Party membership card, after being a member for more than twenty years. He did not want to remain in the same party organization with the vice-president after he had failed to apologize or at least to admit what he had done.

Leaving the Communist Party was a bold deed, particularly since my father took the step before the mass secession from the Party began. As a matter of fact, Paul had set great store by his Party membership. For a long time he had been unable to join the Communist Party; he was afraid of being refused membership because his father, Ignati, had been repressed. That's why he didn't become a Communist until he was forty-two.

Having decided to leave the Party, Paul harnessed himself to my team. Since then, he has taken upon himself the most difficult part of my work—things like dealing with the various administrative offices, taking care of equipment, and doing the necessary driving. The only thing he has never done, or even attempted, is preaching. "It's my business what and how I feel, and I can't talk about it in public," Father confided to me.

Preaching and Learning

To preach in public is not easy, particularly if all the people around you have known you since childhood. "How can it be?" they will ask. "Only yesterday she was just like all of us, but today—just imagine—she's preaching. Is it just acting? Has she gone off her head?"

During the service in which I was consecrated a pastor, I noticed, in spite of my agitation, someone in the hall with a huge pair of field glasses. *Who could be so inquisitive that she wanted to see everything in detail?* I wondered. It turned out to be my cousin Yelena Pasynkova. We had been out of touch for twenty years. Immediately after the service she telephoned Mother and babbled excitedly, "Aunt Raya, do you know that your Lydia has gone off her head?"

Mother jumped up in alarm. "What happened? When?"

"Just today!" said Yelena, in a sympathetic tone of voice. "Didn't you know? She's agreed to become a pastor. It's not done like that—in a twinkling and you're a pastor! She's got schizophrenia!"

"Ah, this!" Mother sighed with relief. "I thought something had really happened. As for Lydia, she's been in the church for more than a year already."

"Oh," said Yelena, disappointed. "I thought they'd just suggested it today and she had agreed at once. Well, now I understand."

But evidently she understood very little. She had to see for herself. So she began to attend the services and even came to our Bible classes. I had never had a more attentive listener. Yelena never missed a single class and she took notes painstakingly. Then she would phone me and for hours try to clear up the details of a lesson or a sermon, for she took notes of the sermons, too. She was trying to make certain that I was in my right mind. I don't really know what she decided, because she no longer attends the church.

Fortunately, most parishioners were compassionate. When they listened to sermons they remembered their childhoods and the legacy of the old people in their lives. When our church members stopped being ashamed of sharing their emotional experiences, their life stories, family traditions, and tragedies, it turned out that many of them had known God since early childhood. They remembered their praying grandmothers, the icons in their village houses, their own journeys, full of pain and astonishing patience.

As they did so, I saw that my own life experiences were not that unusual. The spiritual life of my parishioners proved to be so full, so rich, that as I listened, I cried and laughed together with them. *My God, how deeply they feel! How they believe in Thee!* Who taught them? I never taught Russian Methodists, believe me! I learned from them. They know more than I do, they feel more deeply, they are ready to share everything unstintingly. They are a source of strength, inspiration, and support for me.

6.

THE BIRTH OF NEW CHURCHES

Our church was not the only one Dwight Ramsey helped to develop. Through the help of the Church Development Program, funded by five of the largest United Methodist churches in the United States, new churches appeared in St. Petersburg, Moscow, and Sevastopol. All of them were born through the efforts of my Ekaterinburg* members. We affectionately called them "baby churches." They all began to function without any financial support. They depended on God and also on the enthusiasm, faith, and self-sacrifice inherent in all Russians—Russians like Roman Tselner.

I met Roman Tselner quite "by chance" in February 1991. I was returning from the Sheremyetovo International Airport in Moscow, having failed to meet Dwight and the delegation from Shreveport. This team, under David Stone's leadership, was planning to spend time in Moscow and also visit Sverdlovsk again. I had come to Moscow by plane especially to meet them, because we were worried about Dwight: he had had surgery only eight days earlier and was rushing his recovery. We thought his coming was heroism bordering on madness. In Russia after operations like his, patients stay in the hospital for twenty days.

What has happened to them? I wondered. All kinds of horrors crossed my mind when they didn't get off the plane. As I boarded the bus to go back to Moscow, my mind was occupied with worry and fear. I paid little attention to

---

* Sverdlovsk changed its name back to its pre-Revolutionary name about the time of our land's dedication.

finding a seat except for the fleeting thought, *I hope I don't find myself beside a man; I don't want to be pestered.* Then suddenly I was sitting beside a short, dark-haired man, even though there were several other vacant seats. Roman told me later that, seeing me standing in the aisle, he had decided to test his rather remarkable hypnotic abilities! *Sit next to me!* he commanded mentally, stopping my attempts to choose the person I would sit beside.

In the four years since then, Roman has been my friend and helper. Whatever happens, day or night, rain or snow, in Moscow or in Leningrad, Roman will listen to my wildest requests and just say: "Well, with you, it seems, I'll not die in my bed!" It has become a sort of sign or natural law for him and his friends: "If Lydia and Dwight appear on the horizon, it's the end of normal, peaceful life." At Roman's request his friends have also helped us, doing it mostly for nothing and without sparing time or effort.

In a strange and wonderful way, God sent extraordinary people like Roman Tselner, who has a high position with the St. Petersburg telephone company, across my path. Everything I and later my sister Irina managed to achieve in Leningrad—now St. Petersburg—was due in large part to the efforts of this witty man, the most interesting and decent of all decent people. Where will you get a car, if all the cars of the town seem to be in one long line for gasoline, waiting for hours? What driver will agree to give you a lift if you are standing beside your car with a dead motor? Who will find you a hotel room if there is no accommodation anywhere? Who will work all through the Christmas holidays so you will not miss the humanitarian aid sent from Great Britain for your church? Who will meet you and all your friends and parishioners at the train station or the airport? Roman Tselner.

I'm writing about Roman as one of the best Russian Methodists, though he has never become a full member of any Methodist church, if you mean membership according to *The Book of Discipline*. But Roman is a true Methodist because he gives our church his gifts, his presence, his services, as well as his loyalty, his love, his enthusiasm (the last two are not listed in *The Book of Discipline!*).

Perhaps without Roman there would have been no Methodism here in Russia. Of his own free will he has been helping us to draw our laden cart along the road we have chosen, while inspiring us with his jokes and inimitable smile. Roman's natural humor, his sensitivity, and his great respect for my ministry have meant a lot to me.

St. Petersburg

At Dwight's request, my sister Irina moved to St. Petersburg in order to help develop the First United Methodist Church there. She had been an indispensable help in Ekaterinburg, where she began women's and children's programs, and practically became the founder of the first Methodist school when it started in the small rooms of a hostel.

With her great organizing experience, Irina was afraid of nothing. But she couldn't foresee having to start from ground zero. No Methodist community in St. Petersburg had developed. The first interested people who had earlier signed the organization petition dispersed. And there were other difficulties.

Tatiana Peretolchina, who later became one of our Ekaterinburg parishioners, had given us the address of her aunt in St. Petersburg, as a possible place where Irina could stay. But the address proved to be wrong and Irina was faced with having to spend the night out of doors. Roman, who had met her at the airport in his car, patiently traveled up and down streets with similar-sounding names, but to no avail. Finally he could stand it no longer. He brought Irina to his office and his co-workers managed to find Maria Mikhailovna Volkova's phone number. It turned out she had not been informed of her guest's arrival!

With that inauspicious beginning, Methodism was born for the third time in this wonderful city on the Neva, where the true but forgotten spirit of Methodism had once reigned. Most of the people reviving it never realized how crucial their role was. Maria Mikhailovna might have refused to shelter Irina, who was no relative of hers. She had only one 9' x 15' room. It would be difficult for anyone to live in such a small room with a stranger for a year. Maria had almost no knowledge of the church. She was a former Communist and a veteran of World War II, though she didn't look her age. But she had formerly lived in Sverdlovsk, our hometown. That was, perhaps, the only thing she and Irina had in common. But she allowed Irina to stay with her.

That year of living in a new place with people who were at first complete strangers was a good school for Irina. One of the actions she and Maria Mikhailovna took, as the church developed slowly, was to visit libraries, telling librarians and readers about Methodists. People were impressed that the Methodist Church had existed in St. Petersburg before the Revolution. Miraculously, Maria and Irina met people who even remembered the name of the church and where it was, on 10th Line of Vasilyevski Ostrov, an island in the Neva River! It was there in house N. 37 that the chapel of the Methodist Church had once existed. The house was destroyed during the bombings of World War II. There had also been a shelter and an educational center. George Simons, the district superintendent and editor of *The Christian Advocate,* had lived in the house opposite the church. Inside that house, on the third floor, I saw what remained of the church's stained-glass panels. The delegations brought here by Dwight were quite excited at these discoveries!

In this house I met an old woman who had been a janitor for the church, who told me about the chapel and the old Methodists. The remembrance of that history and the atmosphere of genuine excitement and interest helped to restore Methodism in St. Petersburg again! Little by little, people began to join with Irina—people who had endured the horrors of the repressions and the German blockade of their beloved Leningrad, who had not forgotten the artillery barrages that had destroyed so much of the city, or the thousands of corpses.

When Irina first moved to St. Petersburg, she had no thought of preaching. She was just there to create a community. But one day I got an unexpected phone call from her. "Lyda," she said, "I've preached today! Somebody must do it, and here no one else can." So for a year Irina preached every Saturday, continued her visiting to develop the church, and attended the Logos Seminary that had been started in St. Petersburg by a group of American pastors. She would get up at five o'clock in order to be on time for classes, since she lived a long way from the seminary. To get there she had to cross a vacant lot in the dark, in a dangerous area where people were robbed and murdered every day. No one was surprised to hear gunshots every night, so she always carried a can of mace in her pocket.

Once Maria Mikhailovna was attacked just as she got to her doorway. Her bag was snatched, along with the keys to the flat and her war veteran's certificate—a very important document, which gave the owner the right to buy some items of food at a discount. "I suppose it's because of the church," was Maria's frightened comment. Again Roman Tselner came to their rescue. He changed not only the locks to the apartment but also the doors themselves.

I used to live peacefully and quietly, Maria must have thought. Such thoughts probably occurred to Irina as well. She was now living in a damp, cold climate that was bad for her health. Her feet were wet all the time because her boots soon became worthless in the constant rain and snow, and it was impossible to buy new ones. She could not stay home in bed: if Maria Mikhailovna, with her diabetes, did not stay at home but made the rounds of her friends, old and new, inviting them to the church, then Irina could not let herself relax either.

As one of the first Methodists in Leningrad, Maria Mikhailovna's method never failed. She had never liked to waste her time by sitting with the old women on a bench near the apartment building doorway and gossiping. But now she went up to them with a gentle reproach. "Well, what are you sitting here for? Don't you know that the 'Methodical' church has opened? Come every Saturday evening to our meeting, and don't try to find any excuses!" Almost invariably one or more of the women would show up the next Saturday.

The secret of Maria's influence was her authority among the women of the neighborhood. They had all worked together in the same plant for many years. She had also been the head of her company's Communist Propaganda Committee. People had gotten used to obeying Maria. These elderly women who came to the church on Saturday later became faithful members. Maria and Irina cooked meals for them in their small apartment and visited them in their own homes. The hearts of the women were melted by the love and care, and they learned to give their time and love to others.

Church Conferences

In the past few years the Methodist community has continued to grow. In May 1993, four Russian Methodist churches, three choirs from Russia and America, and four Russian pastors met in St. Petersburg. It was a festive occasion that turned into a competition of Methodist choirs! The guests included the church and choir members from the Moscow church whose pastor, Ludmila Garbuzova, was also born and grew up in Sverdlovsk-Ekaterinburg; the Centenary College choir from Shreveport; and parishioners from Ekaterinburg with our beautiful church choir. Irina was in charge of one of the meetings, her first experience in leading such a large service. Andrei Poopko, the pastor of the Methodist church from Pushkin, a suburb of St. Petersburg, preached at that service.

This was the second grand service of its kind in Russia. The first was an Easter celebration in Moscow in 1992, which was broadcast as "East Meets West—Moscow and Shreveport." This Easter service was held with the blessing of the Patriarch of the all-Russia Orthodox Church, and was the first serious declaration of our existence and purpose. Methodists from many countries came to that service. But the greatest number came from Ekaterinburg. The Methodists from the Urals came with their families, bringing with them the spirit of our church—the spirit of revival, unity, and love.

Before that Easter service a corner of Red Square had been set off for our group. We had just gotten there when we saw on the opposite side of the square, in front of the Hotel Russia, a crowd of people with red flags and placards. "Yankees, get out of Russia!" we read as the demonstrators began to move toward us. "Let's defend children from the influence of the West!" "Russia for Orthodox believers!" The "patriots," apparently hired by someone for this action, were obviously drunk and were holding the placards with difficulty.

"Shield the children!" one of us shouted, and we closed ranks, forming a semicircle around our children. Then, suddenly, the pure boyish voices of Yuri Bondar's choir members began singing behind our backs, seeming to raise a protective dome over us. Though the Methodist church had no building of its own in Russia then, it suddenly acquired a temple; all of us, the ordinary people united by one Faith, became that temple.

"What do you teach the children, sectarians?" Through the singing, we could hear the shouts of the aggressive men and women.

"Listen, they are singing in Russian," someone answered calmly. "This is Russian music." This argument, or possibly the purity that surrounded us, cooled the attackers. Some of them inconspicuously disappeared in the crowd and others, still holding high the now ludicrous slogans, moved back across the Square.

Moscow

At that Easter service, the First United Methodist Church of Moscow was represented by a youth choir, which played a key role in the service. Ludmila Garbuzova, the pastor of the church, is a professional musician. This short, dark-haired, attractive woman impressed me with her energy and optimism from the first time I met her in January 1992. Her spirit is as strong as her personality. She lived with her seventeen-year-old daughter Julia and had to be both mother and father for her.

Perhaps it won't surprise you if I tell you that Ludmila was born and educated in Sverdlovsk, where she studied music with Yelena Tishenko's mother, a musician. Obviously Russian Methodism has the Ural spirit!

Before becoming a Methodist pastor, Ludmila Garbuzova was a Russian Orthodox choir director. She and her choir received several awards and had invitations to visit a number of different countries. As she became interested in Methodism, she was faced with a real problem—to follow her career or to take an unknown way—a way full of difficulties, misunderstandings, and danger. The Spirit and her faith moved her to choose this way.

Ludmila started the church around the youth choir, all of whom supported their favorite teacher. So the First United Methodist Church of Moscow got the nickname "the singing church." And here history came alive. The early Methodists in Russia, before the October Revolution, had a similar name—"singing Methodists." The church began worshiping in the District Music School building, not far from where Ludmila lived. The hall, seating about three hundred, had beautiful stained-glass windows and looked like a real sanctuary.

Unfortunately, Protestantism wasn't very welcome there and it wasn't easy for Ludmila to keep up her good relations with the school after her conversion. One day she and her members were extremely frightened by the anger and hatred exhibited when Orthodox believers visited their worship service and tried to interrupt and ruin the service. Eventually the church had to leave that building.

Ludmila's spirit and tolerance, however, drew a lot of other Orthodox Christians to her, people who loved Ludmila personally, and loved her church as well. Ludmila wanted to make the church comfortable for different kinds of people. Her two-bedroom apartment became a church, a shelter, and a soup kitchen for elderly women, whom she cooked for, warming their hearts by love.

Ludmila in Moscow and Maria and Irina in St. Petersburg used their own limited financial resources for their ministries. That is why, when we received humanitarian aid from the United States, we tried to share with our baby churches. They had nothing! Yet whenever we traveled to Moscow, my members and I always stayed with Ludmila and her daughter. Their patience was endless. We were always welcomed and hosted with smiles and delicious meals. Hundreds of people came through Ludmila's house and heart.

Sevastopol

One of those who was with us for the Moscow celebration was Ivan Kozlov. Ivan, Irina, and I had grown up together in Sverdlovsk, where our parents were friends. Irinka and Ivan used to sit side by side in their prams, looking like twins with their blond curls, while their mothers discussed world problems on a bench. The history of Methodism in Russia has the rare chance to preserve a photo of three future pastors sitting together in a boat in the middle of a lake, wearing identical calico underpants! About twenty years later Valery and Galina Kozlovy, Ivan's parents, moved to Sevastopol in the Crimea. Valery was in the Armed Forces, and after he resigned with the rank of lieutenant-colonel, he moved to the Black Sea town where Ivan later joined them.

We lost touch with Ivan for a long time, but one day, out of the blue, he phoned to say that he was going to visit us. Though he was a grown man, the curls still lying in ringlets on his shoulders reminded us of the former darling Vanechka. Irishka and Mother, interrupting each other, began to tell him about what had happened to me and our family. Ivan kept glancing at me, his eyes narrowed ironically. "And do you really believe?" he asked at last.

That question always stymied me. "Red-tape" officials from the City Soviet usually asked me that, thinking they had a right to ask any questions they wanted. Their tone of voice was always that of a healthy man addressing a sick woman. So inwardly I bristled up at Ivan's question, and for a long time I mistrusted him, thinking his frequent visits to Ekaterinburg were just idle curiosity. But I was wrong. Ivan came to the dedication of our land and had a long talk with Dwight, where I was the interpreter. That was how I got to know Ivan's story and his spiritual suffering. In September 1991, when I saw Ivan among the 132 people waiting to be baptized, I was not surprised. Neither was I surprised when he asked Dwight to found a Methodist church in the Crimea.

Dwight and I came to Sevastopol in October 1992. Getting to this town, a base on the Black Sea for military submarines and warships, has always been a problem. Even those of us who are citizens of Russia had to get a special permit. Once my mother, who had traveled to Crimea on business, decided to visit her friend Galina, Ivan's mother, in Sevastopol. If it hadn't been for a fortunate coincidence, she would have only been able to talk with Galina through the man on duty at the admission control station. The two friends would not be allowed to be together even for a minute. But the man on duty happened to be a former citizen of Sverdlovsk. So he let my mother enter the closed area of Sevastopol on his own responsibility. You can imagine, then, how difficult it was for a foreigner to get permission.

Dwight Ramsey appeared to be the first American allowed to enter Sevastopol. His documents were covered with resolutions and signatures of nine high-ranking officials. When Ivan met us at the Sympheropol Airport, about four hours' drive from Sevastopol, he was exhausted after running to all the departments, and could hardly believe that his marathon was over!

Traveling to Sevastopol by car, we passed through the beautiful Crimean countryside. I saw roses blooming in late autumn for the first time. The sea I had missed so much was calm and mirror-like. We were following the same route that Empress Catherine II (Ekaterina) had once traveled. The places where she had stopped bore unusual names in commemoration of her visit. One of the names astonished me, Chistencoyeh, which means "Clean." Stopping here, Catherine had washed herself in a Russian bath house especially prepared for her. Happy and refreshed, she came out of the bath house and exclaimed: "Yah chistencayah!"— I am clean.

The public worship service took place in the House of Culture. The hall was almost full. Valery and Galina Kozlovy, Ivan's parents, were there with Ivan's sister Velya and her children. That first evening we received a lot of notes with questions that we tried to answer after the service. Some were difficult; others were frankly aggressive; some came from Pentecostal believers who attended the service. It was a good learning experience for me, though a rather difficult one.

The next day there was another service, which was attended only by those in sympathy with us—Methodists and interested people. At the end of the meeting we held a baptismal service. Immediately after the service, Dwight, Ivan, and I were scheduled to fly to Samara—formerly Kujbysev—on the Volga River, to take part in the first conference of all-Russian Methodist pastors and lay leaders. But there were far more people than we could possibly baptize in the time we had. And when we saw the pleading looks of those whom we weren't going to get to, we decided to continue with the baptisms and ignore our scheduled flight and all the other problems our sudden decision involved. The women and children who stood waiting in front of us were the most important concern for us at that moment. Their gratitude still follows us. Anna Arkhipova, a teacher in Sevastopol, wrote us later, "O Lord! You brought us together, You breathed new life into me after baptism. You united us again!"

But sooner or later all things come to an end, and Dwight and I had to leave Sevastopol. Ivan was to develop the church on his own. He had no official support, no means whatever, but he found an original solution. He sold his land on the waterfront for cash ($2,200 U.S.), in order to leave his job as an architect and devote himself full time to the church. He felt he was able to help people, both his friends and strangers, to fill the spiritual vacuum in their souls. He already knew that it was possible, as we had also come to know.

The Sevastopol church became very special for the Ekaterinburg Methodists, just as Ludmila Garbuzova's church in Moscow had earlier. Four members of our church once traveled together to Sevastopol for a visit because they knew how difficult they had found it on their own. Tamara Alekseeva, Tatiana Tomakh (wife of Vladimir Tomakh, who had helped me register the church), Galina Pervushina, and Rudolf Streletsky set out for Sevastopol by car, in spite of a heavy snowstorm in Ekaterinburg. They were glad for one another's presence on the long and difficult trip to the warm Crimea. They brought love and hope to their sisters and brothers in sharing their faith and talking about their church in Ekaterinburg. Our church became for the Sevastopol Methodists what the Broadmoor United Methodist Church in Shreveport was for us—a source of strength and patience.

On this trip, Tamara Alekseeva got to visit with her sister Lydia, whom she hadn't seen for many years. Not only was Sevastopol a closed city, but as perestroika—the restructuring of the Soviet Union—took hold, it was difficult and sometimes impossible to travel from one republic to another because of the growing divisive nationalism. A year later, when Lydia knew she was dying, the first person she phoned was Ivan. Tamara was unable to get to Sevastopol in time for the funeral, but it was a comfort to know that Ivan had been there for her sister in her final days. The burden of Tamara's bereavement was shared by the Methodists of both churches. Her grief was our grief.

It is astonishing how many people were brought together by Methodism: relatives and acquaintances who had not seen one another for decades, old friends, even former enemies. Christianity entered our souls, changing us. Methodism proved to be surprisingly "just right" for us, helping us become aware that we are people, human beings, just as the Lord Himself, not the state, created us. Methodism helped us regain our dignity and live patiently. Against the background of universal disappointment and panic, Russian Methodists looked strange with their unaffected smiles and openness. People used lots of epithets to describe us: "crazy," "not all there," "doltish," "has a screw loose," "a little touched." But it looked like the process was infectious; though each church began with only a few persons, the message kept spreading.

I can hardly believe how many events have occurred during the short period of five years. But then five years is long enough for a small child to absorb almost everything that will come in handy later on in life. From a helpless baby he grows into a little child, whose parents have put into him everything he may need in his life. That was what happened to Methodism in Russia. It absorbed not only what our American Methodist friends had lavishly shared with us, it also took in the pre-Revolutionary features of Russian Methodism: sincerity and intellectual culture. In addition, it imbibed what has always made the Russian soul mysterious: humility and pride, anxiety about their children and the willingness to sacrifice themselves for the sake of their future; grief over their dead and gratitude for them. Methodism in Russia at long last was restored to life after more than sixty years—and so swiftly that it could only be God's plan.

7.

THE STRUGGLE TO LOVE

*I*n October 1992, during one of Dwight's visits to Russia, I told him about a vision I had while I was praying. In my vision I had seen myself swiftly and confidently going through a suite of brightly lit and splendidly furnished rooms. I passed through one room, then a second . . . and after I passed through a tenth high-ceilinged room, I entered a round hall with a domed ceiling. Here I turned into a pigeon and began confidently soaring upwards toward the dome, flapping my wings. I enjoyed flying—my new gift.

Dwight interpreted my vision as a revelation of death. That interpretation did not suit me. "You are wrong," I told him—probably for the first time daring to disagree with my teacher. On the contrary, I felt the Lord had singled me out and had prepared something very important for me.

However, over the next eighteen months my health began to fail. I wondered if perhaps Dwight's interpretation of my vision had indeed been correct.

Increasingly, I had difficulty getting up in the morning. Several times while I was preaching I came close to losing consciousness. My pulse rate rose to 130, and I felt dizzy most of the time. Although my soul was singing—God was talking through me—physically, I felt wretched. I began to have allergic shocks, one after another. My face swelled monstrously and my lips stretched grotesquely, my tongue grew numb and I could hardly breathe. After six such attacks, I lived in extreme dread of the next, fearing it would be the last.

One day, when I had a bit of strength, I timidly asked God: "Why? What is the reason for these attacks?" I desperately needed to find an answer to this question. Some of the church members were starting to blame me for my health problems. "Good Christians are never ill!" they told me.

Over the next months I was tested by many doctors both in Russia and in the United States, but none of them could find any physical cause for my symptoms. "You're the healthiest person in the world," I was told.

"What's wrong with me, then?" I asked.

"Stress."

Stress! I never knew that stress could nearly kill people. But I was too vulnerable, too sensitive. I tried to take all my parishioners' pain as my own. I wanted to solve all their problems at once. Because I was ready to sacrifice myself for them, I sinned. I needed to hear from someone that Jesus had already made the sacrifice. I needed to hear that word again and again. Because as I read about the martyrs and saints in the books I'd bought, I decided I needed to follow them—sacrifice was the only right way for real Christians.

Under Scrutiny

As I began to examine my life, trying to understand myself, I could see that where I had tried to live "by rule" before, now I was even more afraid of stumbling. My parishioners, having chosen a woman as their pastor, were very exacting in their expectations of me. And they were right. This was the first time in Russia that a woman had become a priest, a pastor. At that time we didn't yet know the difference between a pastor and a priest, so they were identical concepts for us. And because I was called a pastor, the congregation expected me to make sacrifices, to act in accordance with the traditions they were used to in the Orthodox church.

For one thing, priests fasted, eating and drinking nothing before baptizing and giving Communion. The parishioners were seriously concerned that I should conform to my priestly "order." Some were dissatisfied with the fact that I wore makeup; others tried to find out my personal habits. They even worried about my bodily functions. In the Orthodox church a woman is considered unclean during her menstrual periods; so how may a woman pastor be allowed to baptize or give Communion then?

These people had just begun to hope, to find their connection with God, after long years of suffering and separation from Him. So it was natural for them to be very strict concerning the person who was to baptize them and, especially, their children. They wanted everything to be done right. So they watched me carefully and waited impatiently to see "improvements" in areas that concerned them.

As a result I felt trapped. I had already made my choice to be God's person, a pastor. I couldn't be the former Lydia. So I felt it necessary to be more strict with myself. My grandfather's example was always in my mind. Subconsciously I could feel what my parishioners expected from me: self-denial and stoicism. Because they brought to the church all their aspirations and prayers, they enriched Methodism; the Russian Methodist church absorbs the different traditions brought to it. My lot was to be worthy of the trust that my parishioners had given me as a gift.

But even people with identical ideas can't become a church at once just by getting together. Even the best of families have their disagreements. If I had understood that then, I might have avoided much of the stress and disappointments! We Russians were taught at school, "The family is the cell of society." That certainly held true for us. Our Methodist church, like a family, was a mixture of everything—good and bad, tragic and comical.

In the comical vein, some folk actually took our church for a theater. I began to realize that, for many people, attending church was like attending a play. There was no other experience of the kind available! The church became a place where people went once a week "to see and be seen"—to have an emotional experience together, to cry together, to criticize the actors (the pastors), to discuss their hairstyles and clothing.

Then again, Russian people couldn't conceive of a church apart from a building, a sanctuary. There is no church without a church building. That's why many parishioners at first behaved the way they were used to behaving in any other public place—arriving late, talking during the sermon, eating during the service. It was not their fault. Even if people had experienced an Orthodox church service, it didn't help them to know how to behave in the former Communist center where our services were held. We had no icons, no priest.

"True, there is a woman dressed in a robe to look something like a priest. She talks about God and seems to be talking sincerely, without consulting any notes. But how the devil do we know what she's like?" If someone didn't know the time and effort I put into my ministry, our services looked just like that—rather absurd and incongruous.

People came to worship and to pray in the enormous fifteen-hundred-seat hall of the Political Education Center, where for years they had come to study at the school of Marxism-Leninism. They came to the same hall where an enormous portrait of Lenin used to hang; now candles were burning on a simple altar. For some it was just a change of scenery on the same stage. I was just another lecturer, or an actress. For others, I was a monster, a werewolf!

"Do you think you are a saint?" one parishioner once demanded of me. She was constantly bothered by the question of what her place was in the church. The Christian faith, in her and her supporters' opinion, had done her an injustice. She had more right to be in my place. "You aren't any better than any one else," she added. "You aren't Jesus Christ."

Over the previous two years I had forgotten my childish misgivings about the church. I had begun to trust everyone, whether friends or enemies. So when conflicts began to emerge I was not ready. I was trying to follow the Bible. But as I read the Bible, I stumbled over many passages and had a lot of questions. However, there was no one who could enlighten me, and I couldn't seem to discuss my questions over the phone with Dwight. I had no library, only four or five books and all of them in English. In addition, I could only find time for reading at night. Videotapes of the services from Broadmoor Church in Shreveport helped; I could review them over and over, learning from them each time.

Some time later, I found another solution. I began to buy rare and rather expensive Orthodox books. They opened for me the hitherto unknown world of Russian saints and half-forgotten churchmen, whose names had been painstakingly obliterated from our national memory. Their influence on my soul, craving for knowledge, was fruitful. In them I found answers for many of my questions and began to get rid of my doubts.

Conflicts over Privilege

During 1992, however, my doubts and questions resurfaced, and at that particular time I felt spiritually bankrupt. The Lord was testing me again. I did not know then that God never sends more trials than a person can bear. The criticisms of me and the church were mounting, and there were periods when disappointments made my heart sink. I kept waiting for the next crisis. *Who will be the next to betray me?* was my constant question. I believed that nothing good would happen—and my presentiments came true!

The problem lay with my expectations of the church. I never expected that I would suddenly find myself in the center of politics and struggle—in the church! When I realized that I had problems not only in the world as a whole—

with the Russian government, with the city—but also in the church, I was devastated. When I opened my eyes in the morning, I regretted that I was awake. I didn't want to live. The church was too sacred a place for conflict. But here the problems were—and I had no expertise in resolving them, no experience of handling conflict. No doubt that was one of the reasons the problems befell me.

One major area of conflict came in connection with the humanitarian aid we received from our brothers and sisters in the United States, from our friends in Broadmoor Church and also from other churches across the U.S. Never had our city seen the like of what came in the huge Ruslan, the government's largest transport plane (provided free), which flew in to Ekaterinburg on April 21, 1992, filled with medical supplies and boxes of food, both in bulk and individually wrapped as gifts. The items of food were so beautifully packed and wrapped that many of the children and older people kept the bright wrappings and the containers as a reminder of the generous gifts.

Our parishioners worked at unloading the plane, along with some servicemen who were asked to help by Victor Peretolchin, a parishioner. Victor also provided the trucks to take the food to the central distribution point, the Diagnostic Center, where several of our parishioners worked. The center allowed us to use their storehouses gratis. After the plane was emptied and everything was transported to the center, our parishioners delivered the heavy boxes, twenty kilos or approximately forty-five pounds each, to apartments in houses without elevators. The surprised and grateful sobs of the old women who had lost all hope of getting any assistance from anywhere, the sincere gratitude of war veterans, and the joyful laughter of children were reward enough.

Many of the old women laughed like children as they examined the completely new and fantastic items of food from overseas. But their grateful excitement turned to fear—were these boxes given to them just to make camera shots for a film, and then to be taken away? It had happened before!

In one of the half-ruined houses, we visited a woman and her fourteen-year-old daughter. Both of them were disabled and were reduced to living like beggars. The woman was so emaciated that her age was undefinable. When they opened their box and the girl saw the chocolate inside, she cried out in delight, "Mum, Mum! Look! It's sugar!" The mother gave no reaction—she had never seen chocolate before. Many of the recipients saw chocolate for the first time in their lives.

As we visited the old, forgotten women, I began to have doubts again. *Where is justice?* These hungry, poverty-stricken women had never been lazy. They had worked hard for thirty, forty, fifty years. And now nobody wanted them. *Where is the Lord?* I wondered. Most of them had been atheists, but when they were given the food, they crossed themselves clumsily, and hastily repeated, "Thank God! Thank God!" They understood at once that this aid did not come from their native land, their own government for which they had toiled all their lives, from youth to old age. The aid came from the church, from believers in the United States, from the country they had long considered their enemy. It came, in fact, from the people they had been afraid of for years. Now, getting these parcels, they remembered that during World War II Americans had sent them food parcels and clothing. One elderly woman, a former teacher, suddenly remembered receiving a nice dress when she had been a little girl. I remembered my grandfather telling us about the splendid American "pork stew"—canned pork—he had eaten. I didn't know at the time that I'd later meet Jack Bush in Tennessee, whose father had owned a plant in Sevierville that produced canned pork.

Other recipients remembered other interesting details from those World War II food parcels. One family proudly showed us the box they had saved for almost fifty years that had brought them food from America. Now another American box was put on the shelf beside that one.

Late in the afternoon on the first day of unloading, many of us who had been helping with the unloading and distribution were talking with our American friends in the hotel of the Eye Microsurgery Center. This beautiful white building with an enormous moving eye on its roof was the pride of our town, and our friends had been invited to stay there. Even in the hotel we had to wear sterile white cloth slippers or overshoes over our footwear. A bit dismayed at first, the Americans grew to love and appreciate the well-equipped, up-to-date medical facility. It had been built quite recently, by a Finnish firm, and had taken only two years to construct. By Russian standards that was a fantastic time frame. In Sverdlovsk, construction sites had littered the town with unfinished concrete monsters for twenty years! The Eye Center's unique architecture interested us, because we were in the process of planning our church building.

Unaccustomed to the businesslike approach, we Russians felt as though we were tourists in this center, with its faultless cleanliness, its pleasant scent, the friendly, smiling staff, and the numerous computers. The chief, a young, talented, and dedicated surgeon, was perhaps too strict, I thought, on the matter of cleanliness; he fired people much too quickly for what I considered unimportant faults. I didn't realize then that everything is important!

While the others were talking that afternoon, I was dreaming of the good managerial style in our church. I was thinking of all our wonderful helpers, along with all the parishioners who shouldered the burden of those first years, all the wise and spiritually rich people of our church. *Actually,* my thoughts ran on, *we need a different method of management, more acceptable for the church—the way of forgiveness and trust.*

Suddenly my thoughts were interrupted by the sight of my father at the other end of the corridor. He had gone home after the tiring day—but here he was, looking pale and agitated.

"We were all taken to the police station!" he said angrily. "Here's the statement." And then he explained.

Our parishioners, exhausted after unloading the plane, had been driven home by the few lucky owners of private cars. One of the men took quite a few in his car, including my father—so many, in fact, that they had great difficulty shutting the car doors. They hadn't gotten very far when they were stopped by a police patrol.

"What are you carrying?" the armed officer asked the driver.

"Nothing," he answered.

"Open the trunk," the officer ordered.

My father got out with the driver as he reluctantly half-opened the trunk lid. My father was struck dumb! There in the trunk was an enormous box containing shampoo, soap, deodorant, and toothpaste. The box had been sent to our church by American pilots from Barcsdale Air Force Base in Louisiana—and its contents were commodities in short supply, in fact impossible to obtain anywhere in Ekaterinburg. Dwight had ordered that only food parcels be given to those who unloaded the plane. This was no food box, in content or size—it was twice as big.

Naturally, the driver "did not know" how that heavy box had gotten into the trunk of his car. And the police were embarrassed; they had nearly arrested a major of the Interior Forces, one of "their own." (He was on the prison board.) But they did draw up a statement of the case. And it was this document Father brought to us as he told us his story.

When the driver's wife, one of our hardest workers, heard Father's story she began to weep. "How can you suspect my husband?" she cried angrily. "He is the most honest man. We've done so much for the church!" The next morning she raised a general alarm among their friends and relatives, and the scandal was hushed up. In fact, I put this unpleasant moment out of my mind, preferring to trust and forgive and offer the other cheek when one was slapped.

The Conflict over Power

The woman whose husband was nearly arrested was brought to the church by my sister Irina in August 1991. She was a hard worker, persistent and ready to do everything, so she soon became a key person. One of my former jobs had been with the Institute of Management, and I tried to put some of those principles to work in the church. A very important principle for me was to share my ideas with staff members so that the ideas would become their own. I did that with this woman. From the start, I always thanked her for everything she did, wanting to make her feel that the church really needed her. Unfortunately, I didn't recognize the first signs of danger.

I did wonder, however, whether the principles of management might not work for Russians, because I began to find my office almost empty, with no church members coming by. What happened was that this staff member became a filter for allowing—or not allowing— people to come in and talk to me. She made the decisions. When someone knocked on my door, she would leave, talk to the person in the corridor very quietly, and then come back into the room to tell me, "No problem. It's been taken care of."

Much later I learned what happened. "We were told," people shared with me, "'Lydia is busy,' or 'Lydia is tired,' or 'Lydia is ill.'" So people got an image of me as either an unattainable star or as a constantly ill person.

The woman also took advantage of the information she got from me. Without asking me, she would phone my partners and friends about her own problems, not about church problems. I learned this one day from a friend in the Russian government, who mentioned that she had called him in my name. Then other people from the city council and the regional government told me the same thing. I was so trustful and naïve. I really didn't expect that she, or anyone, would create a typical socialistic, corrupt system in the church: an "I'll do something for you if you'll do something for me" way of operating. She also played up to important people, greeting them warmly, but she turned her back on ordinary people.

When one of our members left the church, she told me, "I needed a family and new brothers and sisters. But I found myself unimportant to your administrative assistant. When I wanted to ask her something, she just turned her ponytail to me and started to talk with another person. After it happened at least three times, I decided to leave. What kind of people do you have around you, Lydia?"

What kind of people? People who had become corrupted, who weren't there to help the church but to benefit themselves, using the church's name and reputation.

When this woman became my right-hand person, I thought it would be better for the church if my relatives did not serve in the church, remembering "Sultanov House." Only my father stayed on as one of my best helpers. I felt this was the right decision, but it created a lot of problems both in and out of the family.

Another conflict arose when a delegation from our church visited Austria in July 1992. I wasn't with the church members then because of my trip to the United States, so I don't think I have a right to go into detail about the incident. I will just say that it was a typical case of Russians traveling abroad for the first time. In addition, there was a conflict between those who spoke English and those who didn't. Those who knew English were eager to find friends and become "the elite," while the rest of the delegation felt doubly offended. Not only were they left out, but their brothers and sisters, Christians, refused to interpret for them. When they wanted to express their opinions, or to spend time in conversation with Austrians and other foreigners, they were told, "We don't have time for making our own personal contacts!" and "This is work and must be paid for." This obviously led to personal conflicts.

How was it that, after belonging to the same church for a year, the members forgot all the lessons of Christianity and stopped helping one another as soon as they found themselves abroad? At the same time, perhaps it wouldn't have become such a seemingly insurmountable problem for us if someone had explained to all of us that a conflict in a church is quite normal. In a sense it is growing pains—it just happens and passes. Conflict isn't fatal. But unfortunately, no one was on hand to tell us that. It was also sad that this conflict occurred before the eyes of all the Methodist world.

Dwight visited our church as soon as he could after the Austrian visit, and talked frankly with all of us. But it was already too late for some of those who had decided that our church was developing the wrong way.

"This isn't a church," some said. "It's a family business," referring to the part my father played in helping with the affairs of the church.

"European Methodism is different from the one we are developing," said others. "We have it all wrong. Our services are conducted the wrong way."

"We want freedom in the church!" demanded another, more radical group.

When I met with the group that had gone to Austria— and we had sent the best of our parishioners—I saw only thirst for punishment. They were divided by hatred into two groups. Unfortunately, my mother was in one of those groups. As they explained their points of view, each side expected me to be just—or, to be more exact, to condemn the other side. But I disappointed both sides, refusing to listen to either side's complaints. It seemed to me they needed time to cool off, and it was useless to stir up unpleasant memories.

"Time will pass," I told them, "and you will love one another as before. Later on you'll remember only the nice things about the trip." But my words satisfied no one, and now it was I who was being blamed—the pastor who didn't want to listen to her parishioners at a difficult moment.

The result was that several families left the church at once, and the rest of the church was abuzz with talk. Their leaving would be only a beginning, I thought. The negative criticism I sensed from them was very destructive, and I found it extremely hard to preach. I was disappointed—in myself and in the church. I couldn't bring myself to stand in front of the parishioners and speak about love, forgiveness, or patience while I felt their censure, resentment, and unasked questions. I even thought about leaving the church.

One of the problems was that I'm a bad actress—I can't hide my feelings and I am too vulnerable. Then, too, I was an inexperienced preacher, with a limited knowledge of Christian teaching. I lacked theological training, which would have given me some prestige and stature. Some knowledge of psychology would have helped also. But I had none of these. And so all my doubts became very obvious in my sermons. Whether I was right or wrong to do so, my sermons contained my own thoughts, my own suffering, my own tears.

"Love Thy Neighbor as Thyself"

Our Lord foresaw tremendous difficulties for his disciples—including us—in fulfilling the commandment, "Love thy neighbor as thyself." One of them is the question he was asked, "And who is my neighbor?" During this time, I thought a lot about this command and the problem of neighbors. At one point, I began to read a book by Alexander Meyn and was surprised at how closely my thoughts agreed with his. Meyn suggested that Judas, who betrayed Jesus, was his favorite disciple. Jesus trusted Judas with his innermost thoughts, but Judas was a materialist. Money and worldly well-being were the mainstays of his life. Jesus guessed that Judas dipped his hand into the communal purse, but he never reproached him and didn't try to catch him in the act. Moreover, "Jesus knew from the first who were the ones that did not believe, and who was the one that would betray him" (John 6:64). Judas, who loved Jesus, couldn't forgive him when, having refused the kingdom on earth, Jesus urged his disciples to suffer privation for the sake of some unknown and obscure future. But Judas was one of Jesus' neighbors, wasn't he?

And who else was a neighbor of Jesus? Pontius Pilate. Pilate couldn't bring himself to decide, to insist that Jesus was not guilty. Pilate is like the intellectual, educated person, who is really, as we say, "lame in both legs"—that is, living by the principle "it doesn't concern me."

If these were Jesus' neighbors, who could he lean on? Where could he find support? When he called on people to obey the commandment, "Love thy neighbor," he understood the kind of neighbors he was talking about: Judas, Caiaphas, Pilate. When God sent His only Son to earth, He Himself fulfilled the law He left to us: "Love thy neighbor as thyself."

But what does the second part of this law mean—to love our neighbor as ourselves? As I reflected on this second part I asked myself, Who am I, myself? Do I love myself?

At a meeting with first-year students at a technical school, I asked them that question: "Do you love yourselves?" Almost all of them sighed and answered no. How is it that most people don't love themselves? It's difficult not to humiliate another person if you allow yourself to be humiliated. It is practically impossible to feel the pain of another if you beat up on yourself. It's easy to tell a lie if you habitually let others deceive you.

So who are we? The truth is, we are Judas, Caiaphas, Pontius Pilate—a materialist, a rationalist, an ivory-tower intellectual. And there are other, more unpleasant personalities in us. Whichever personality takes the upper hand at a certain moment determines how we react to our neighbors and to the commandment. We determine whether we will betray or conquer the Caiaphas in ourselves, whether we'll say "pardon" when some innocent person's life is in our power, whether Pontius Pilate will become more resolute or will wash his hands after taking part in a crime.

But what about Simon Peter? He is sure to be among our neighbors. And what about the Simon Peter in us, the strong Christian for whom love for God is stronger than his own desires and perhaps even his own life? The Judases and Caiaphases and Pilates among us need Simon Peters. They need people who will love, understand, and support them, people who are ready to share the burden of the cross, the shame and humiliation of their neighbors.

What Kind of Love?

I used to be very fond of aquarium fish. I loved to watch them play, to see how the males frothed up the water. Wonderful thoughts came to me as I watched them. Sometimes I would sit in front of the aquarium, lost in reverie until the wee hours of the morning. Still, I always had time for my friends if they needed me, if something happened and I could help them. But when I began working for the church, I forgot about everything else—my home, family, children, even myself. I did my work willingly, feeling no regrets, taking no notice of time. Then one day I remembered my aquarium. When I walked over to it I saw that the water had evaporated. I looked inside, afraid to imagine what might have happened. There on the bottom were all those dead, dried-up fish that had once been so wonderful and merry. An awful feeling of shame and remorse crept over me.

All of a sudden I understood that while I was helping my neighbors, not many of whom were Simon Peters, the fate of those neglected, dried-up fish could befall my next of kin. At last I understood the second part of the commandment, "Love thy neighbor as thyself." I needed to care for myself and my family. Even now I find this hard, tending to focus on my work and all the needs and tasks people have laid on me, too often forgetting the needs of my family. But then some threat to the children's health or the family's welfare brings me up short and covers me with the same feelings of shame and remorse. This is a constant struggle.

I also came to see that love toward our neighbors must be not only merciful but also strict and exacting. For if we are strict with ourselves, we must take care not to spoil our neighbors with excessive protection, overindulging and corrupting them. A story I read recently in a book of Grimms' fairy tales illustrates this point.

Once a cat and a mouse bought a pot of fat and were discussing where to hide it until winter. "The best place is the church," the mouse decided. "Nobody will ever steal our pot if we hide it under the altar." But soon after that the cat grew hungry, and . . .

After one of the many times I preached about loving our neighbors, one of our parishioners came to me and said, "You teach us that we are to love our neighbors. But my new fur cap was stolen in the church today." Others told me about money and other personal items being stolen. Hearing about the thefts made me feel like the deceived mouse. Even my money was once stolen in the church. I had always thought the church to be a sacred place, that people who opened their souls in church to commune with God would become pure and childlike and defenseless, so that offending one of them is like offending a child.

"If you are deceived for the first time, those who deceived you ought to be ashamed. But if you are deceived the second time, it is you who should be ashamed." That English saying was quoted to me by a church member when I talked about the thefts. In the light of our later relationship, her quoting the saying was ironic. She was our first elderly parishioner. That in itself was remarkable—an elderly, educated person interested in our church. She started coming in 1991, before I returned to Ekaterinburg after little Paul's illness. I was glad to have a new parishioner who also knew English. With the first American delegation's imminent arrival, every English-speaking person was especially important. When I first met her in July 1991, this tall, slender, quiet woman attracted me by her rationalism and reticence.

In November 1991, she visited a friend in the United States and then traveled to Shreveport to visit our sister church. I was happy that she represented our church and I could visualize her meeting with Dwight Ramsey and his congregation. And I appreciated receiving the letters and packages she brought back for me from my friends in Shreveport, along with the assurance of their concern and prayers. I was both embarrassed and deeply moved by the fact that they also sent money. Then Violet handed me a separate envelope of money, saying, "This is for you personally."

"For me? Not for the church?" I asked.

"I don't know," she answered. The sum was large—$120. So I decided it was for the church, of course.

Not long after that her husband had a heart attack and was taken to the hospital. When she told me about it, she also mentioned how difficult it was to buy foodstuffs and that she was short of money. My reaction was a feeling of guilt. It seemed to me that she was reproaching me, implying that my life was much easier than hers. I lived with that feeling the entire week. Then suddenly I thought about the $120 cash gift. I was planning to use it to help pay the teachers at our young Methodist school a bit more. But I decided that she needed money more than anything else, and I'd give her some of that money and make her feel a little easier.

"Thanks," she said, smiling sourly as she accepted the gift of $50. "But, of course, you understand that this is only enough to buy candy!"

The bitterness of this comment stuck like a fishbone in my throat for a long time, because my salary in those days was only $25 a month! Unfortunately, her attitude had repercussions. One Sunday I wore my glasses while I was preaching, because of my shortsightedness, and I was horrified to see the unkind stares of some parishioners. I could feel them glaring at my back even when I stood facing the altar. After that, I began to feel physically sick during services, when I saw the normally reticent elderly woman talking incessantly with her neighbors. Because of the difference in our ages, I felt I could not reprimand or rebuke her. Her attitude made me doubt my abilities; I began to think the level of my preaching was so low it couldn't keep their attention. I suffered a great deal over this. When I talked about my faith candidly, I wanted to be heard— especially when I had opened my heart.

Takers and Givers

During this time my thoughts were continually focused on the church, on unity, and especially on our Methodist school, which opened in 1991. One parishioner expressed the hopes of us all when she brought her children to the school on the first day: "Life has got a new meaning now." But as the days went by, the euphoria evaporated, and after the Christmas holidays were over, everything was sadly different. The teachers began whispering together rather than devoting their time to the children. They were complaining about their low salaries. I couldn't understand their attitude. They got no less than the other teachers in town. But the parents sided with the teachers. "If the church doesn't have enough money," they said, "we don't want the church! It's time to separate."

Then the parents began to have frequent meetings to prepare documents for legally separating the school from the church. But the church had done all the hard work of starting the school and had paid all the expenses for repairing the rented building. At one meeting, a man stood up to shout, "Let Lydia go to America more often and preach in order to earn money for the church. And if she can't, well, let her go and unload freight cars."

While teachers and parents met and talked, they left the children to their own devices. I became very concerned for the children's safety. A little girl from another kindergarten that met in the same building with our school had her finger torn off by a door. I was shaken by the tragedy, concerned lest a similar accident happen to another student.

There were more difficulties. The whole country was going through hard times. Not only was food scarce, but it was next to impossible to buy soap or shampoo, and no one got enough vitamins. As a result, the children became louse-infected, and so did some teachers, and we had to close down the school to disinfect the building. The church was blamed for the lice, not the nurse or the teachers or the parents.

Because many of the parents were our parishioners, the discontent began to spill over into the church, and to other parishioners. Once when I visited the school, I came upon the elderly woman parishioner with a group of parents in a heated discussion—which stopped as soon as they noticed me. In the church itself, groups of activists, both pro and con, would stay in the hall after services, huddled together to talk. In my sermons, I began to talk about tolerance and loyalty.

After I used the word *loyalty* for the first time, the elderly woman remarked maliciously, "This notion bears no relation to the church!" Loyalty was rejected as something beyond our strength and was given no chance to take root. Again I was grieved and distressed, wondering what I had done wrong, what my fault was. I had a hard time understanding the change. After we had worked together with such enthusiasm, such joy, delivering the heavy parcels of food to senior citizens and disabled children, why this estrangement, this hatred?

As I continued to think about the church and its problems, I began to see that the people who needed the church were not primarily those who craved personal contact with Americans. It was the people who had been seeking God who found the church necessary. Because they were alone they had failed to find Him. These were the people who were ready to give more than they hoped to receive. And, I realized, the majority of our parishioners were such people.

Those who had come to the church hoping to get something—privilege, material aid, contact with Americans—left. They left when they understood that the church entails, first and foremost, the readiness to make sacrifices. It is not a trade union, where members are accustomed to receiving material aid, or free accommodations in vacation resorts, or trips abroad. The church is not a correspondence club where one gathers pen pals. Quite a large number of people left, including whole families, even though we needed their assistance badly. Yet every time we had visitors from abroad, they showed up again! It was a mystery to me how they learned about our visitors, but always, there they were after at least a six-month absence. Perhaps they got letters from friends they had made in the church.

The conflict affected all of us who had come to the church seeking unity, friendship, brotherhood, and faith in God. Attendance at services now was between seventy and eighty, in contrast to the 270 or so who used to come on Sunday, and the ninety or one hundred who came on Wednesday evening. The decline was upsetting. But gradually new people came to the church. The atmosphere of the hall cleared up and it was easier to preach. The new members proved to be real believers. I haven't gotten to know them as well as my first parishioners, but I have learned to love them with all my heart and soul. They came to the church in order to give their time, their scanty means, their hearts. One woman, in those hard times, donated her first pension money to the church. Another gave us videotapes and fax paper—both so expensive that the church couldn't afford to buy them. These two women, together with a third, began to brew medicinal herbs and bring the concoctions to the church in vacuum bottles, for weak parishioners and children. It took them an hour and a half to get to the church, but they refused to use the church van, even during the most severe frosts. "We don't want to waste fuel," they said.

When still another woman lost her job, she came to the church every day for three months, to do whatever needed to be done—all without pay. One man helped with the bookkeeping, when I needed it, and drew up all our legal documents. He even helped with the preaching. He did all that, not because he had nothing to do. In order to feed his family he was working at six different places! A woman began to offer medical consultations to our parishioners twice a week. After a year, she decided to organize a family doctors service in our church, and a man joined her. Using up-to-date medical equipment, they were able to help so many members, not only examining them but curing them.

Thus parishioners themselves, with God's assistance, made our church their home, a place they are eager to return to again and again. And not because the pastors are good, but because real love lives in the church.

Russian people had seldom been given such kind attention. And our parishioners responded by doing what they could for the church. The older women, some of them nearly blind, knitted scores of socks and mittens for the children of the church and for women prisoners. They collected money for our building fund and donated their own "widow's mite" wholeheartedly. A ninety-two-year-old parishioner, whose father had been shot in 1934, asked me when she could bring her money for the church construction. This shy, truly cultured woman wears thick-lens glasses and a hearing aid. Knowing her lack of means, I tried to dissuade her by saying, "No, don't bring it. It's too cold and icy and you might fall." But she came anyway, and gave us 1,000 rubles when her pension was only 14,000 rubles.

Thus Russian Methodists, old and young, began to learn the meaning of the word *pledge,* as well as what it means to be a member of the church in deed as well as in word. The Lord sent these parishioners to me as a consolation, and because of them I did not leave the church, though they never sensed this treacherous thought, which visited me more and more often. And whenever it came, some sad or joyful event returned me back to life and made me realize that I could not leave these people, even if I had to spend all my time away from my children and my parents and have no time for myself. These patient, faithful, noble people believed me when I stood in front of them. They accepted me as I was then, just a young woman, an inexperienced pastor.

Conflicts with Other Pastors

One day a man with a pleasant voice telephoned me to introduce himself. "I'm Father Francisk, pastor of the Lutheran church. I've come from ____" and he named a not-too-distant city. "I'd like to meet you. I was advised to get in touch with you by the Religion Department."

When I met him, he was wearing a brown suit and an enormous blue velvet beret, which I found quite absurd. I knew nothing then about the special headdress bachelors of theology wore. We were standing on the street and all passersby turned around to look at us because of that monstrous beret. Besides, it was August and the weather was much too warm to think of wearing any kind of headgear. I brought the pastor to the Znanie Society office where I used to work, and my colleagues' eyebrows shot up in amusement.

We found an empty room, and for about two hours I listened to Father Francisk's monologue about his own indisputable merits. We were often interrupted by one or another of my former colleagues opening the door to ask, "What on earth are you doing here?" Dazed and stupefied after two hours, I felt faint and could hardly remember why we had met. Suddenly, Father Francisk became aware of my pallor (at that time I no longer wore any makeup) and asked distrustfully if I were fasting. (I was.) He was perplexed by my asceticism.

"As for me," he said proudly, "I love two things: women and having a good meal."

Suddenly he seemed to remember that I was a woman and switched subjects.

"You're not allowed to preach or even teach in the church because you are a woman!" he said firmly. And he began to spout Scripture quotations.

I had thought a lot about this subject. So I asked him frankly, "But who else is there to preach? We don't have a theologically prepared pastor yet."

"Take me!" Father Francisk replied instantly, as if he had prepared his offer of services long ago. "I've got theological education and our church is small. We have no room to spread out. Oh, if only we could open a church in Ekaterinburg!"

I visualized him—self-satisfied and exuding arrogance—standing in front of my dear, self-sacrificing, easily wounded parishioners, and was filled with indignation. *Never!* I said, "And who will teach you what is necessary to do in the Methodist church?"

"You, of course," he answered deferentially.

"If I may teach you, why then may I not teach my parishioners?" I spoke slowly and deliberately, separating each syllable.

Father Francisk thought for a long time. Then, finding no answer, he placed his hands on my shoulders and gave his blessing: "Teach!"

I had another funny encounter at a meeting the town Religion Committee organized. The meeting was held in the expensively furnished, modern office of the Orthodox Church Center, to discuss the construction of a memorial shrine on the spot where the Tsar's family had been murdered. Father John was a former KGB officer and a good bit younger than I. At first, not knowing who and what I was, he playfully flirted with me. When all of us were seated around the table, wine glasses filled with brandy were set before us, and he as the host offered a toast.

"Don't refuse, child," the young priest said to me reproachfully, "when the Lord Himself is filling your wine glass." Somewhat aghast, I didn't say anything, since he was, apparently, on special terms with the Creator. However, when I was introduced as a pastor, Father John couldn't check his irritation. "Lord, what a h-heresy!" he cried, and swallowed another glassful of brandy.

Then, looking me up and down, he loudly introduced me to his staff: "This Lydia is a priest, too, only she wears a skirt. Well, we wear cassocks. A cassock, or a skirt—what's the difference!" But then he went on to quote the scripture about how women ought to behave in the church, the implication being "Put a kerchief on your head and shut up, my dear!"

I could not help reminding him, a bit spitefully, I'm afraid, that he had almost identified himself with our Lord. For a moment I thought I had made him uneasy. But that was probably just naïve wishful thinking. He was not really the kind to be embarrassed. He was focused on the power and the big money going into the building of the shrine, for which people were donating not only money, but icons, gems, and jewelry. Soon after that, the man disappeared from Ekaterinburg with seven emeralds and several rare icons, throwing confusion into the hearts and souls of many people, not just believers.

Coping with the Committee on Religion

It took awhile for us pastors of different churches to understand that we had become a necessary tool in the hands of the politicians. The Committee on Religion had once, on principle, categorically opposed religion. But with the advent of democracy, this advocate of atheism changed its guise, becoming a "kind and helpful" assistant in the registration of new denominations. The freedom now granted to all kinds of churches and sects was astonishing. "White brothers" appeared everywhere, taking teenagers away from their families and turning them into zombies who could not remember anything about their past lives or even their parents. A certain Vissarion appeared on the scene, who claimed to have written a new "New Testament" and who declared himself to be the Christ. He abolished the Lord's Prayer and flooded the country with videotapes of his sermons.

What was the point of allowing all this chaos unless someone thought it was needed? Freedom of religion ended in the legalization of the Russian Orthodox Church as the state church, the implication being that all the other relig-

ions only brought discord, stupefied brains, or bribed parishioners. So the Methodist Church, as well as all other
Protestant churches, was considered a sect. And all the
religion committees of every community were transformed
into committees for the regulation of relations between
religious organizations. ("Regulation" in Russia means destruction.) Thus the bureaucracy was born. First, churches were
allowed to exist. Then it was necessary to create reasons
for misunderstanding among them in order to have something to "regulate." The religion committee workers will
always be important and necessary, therefore they will have
jobs. Since their necessity is evident, how can one dispense
with them!

The freedom with which the representatives of such
committees meddled in our affairs was deceiving. At first it
looked like sincere interest, and any problems seemed to be
just normal ones that could happen in any office. I had no
way to evaluate the constant problems, because I kept away
from politics. Finally, though, I realized something was
wrong when I encountered open and fantastic blackmail. I
was stopped after the service one Sunday and warned by a
parishioner who was a member of the Committee on
Religion, "Lydia, there are awful rumors about you. The
clouds are gathering at the highest level. You're supporting
one of the Russian political parties. Tell me, whom did you
visit recently—I mean, a very important person? Tell me
and we'll try to help you."

For the first time in all my dealings with the committee,
I felt like laughing. Before that, the committee had threatened me with real things—like losing the land given us for
the construction of the church, or eviction from our rented
building without any apparent reason. Their threats
worked: I was always nervous, and the instability affected
my parishioners for whom the church was a refuge from
earthly troubles. But this present accusation was just laugh-

able—the people making the accusation must be daft! How could I financially support a whole political party? It was all nonsense, I thought, and so I didn't add this talk to my list of problems, which were already of cosmic proportions. And that was my mistake.

My next meeting with the Committee on Religion was really comical. Our church was given a building formerly used by a kindergarten so that we could develop a school for disabled children. The previous building, which we had repaired for our Methodist school, had been taken away from us. When we saw this kindergarten building, we nearly cried. The floors had rotted completely through, and on the ground floor there weren't even any boards—you could see through to the oily water several inches deep in the basement, where the water pipes were old and leaky. So the building didn't just need repairing—it would have to be almost completely rebuilt. The financing was to come from the United Methodist Committee on Relief—UMCOR.

As we thought about it, however, we realized that renovating the building would be much too expensive. And we were becoming aware of another, very pressing need. For years we'd followed our governmental policy of hiding our heads in the sand like ostriches, so not to see the growing problems among young people. When we opened our eyes, we saw the problems were enormous. More and more teenagers were committing suicide, running away from home, living on the street. We heard more and more about child abuse and drug problems. And we heard, too, about the increasing number of prisons for teenagers. It would be better, we decided, to create a shelter for teenagers who had no place else to turn. UMCOR agreed to finance the project.

After we remodeled the building, the city bristled up and began to ask, *How could we give such a splendid building to a church? The pastor is such a changeable woman—first she wants to open a school, and then it's a shelter, and tomorrow, who knows what she'll want. And who wants shelters nowadays anyway?* So I got the reputation of being an inconsistent pastor, and a crafty one. People said, "Lydia needs to be controlled. She should make the city council educational board her partner, so they can keep tabs on her." I didn't understand that the game had gone too far until the same "well-wisher" who had come to warn me before appeared in my office.

"Lydia, I must have a private talk with you." For some reason she was whispering.

"I've got no secrets from my colleagues," I replied, refusing to be confidential.

"Lydia, it's very serious. The storm clouds are thickening above your head. Your name is mentioned at the highest level in town. People are displeased with you. They're saying that the building the town transferred to you you've leased to some firm and put the money into your pocket." She was still whispering.

The accusations hurt me, coming as they did after weeks of hard work and little sleep. But almost at once I felt merriment building in me. *How far,* I wondered, *can my "friends'" fantasy take them, when they think of the original state of that building—ruin and devastation everywhere, toilets out of order, no running water?*

With a serious face I answered her. "Yes, it's true. I really am leasing the building."

"To whom?" She jumped up from her chair.

"I've opened a brothel there," I said sarcastically, as it dawned on me that I had gone through this same scenario once before. My answer surprised even me, but I was furious at being accused—again—of something I hadn't done. The last time I had been accused not in a church, but in a police station, which made all that was taking place now seem so much more disgusting and frightful. "How long must this go on?" I asked God.

Help from American Friends

A surprising thing happened when we were distributing the humanitarian aid we had received from the United States among war veterans. My father had been a probationer pilot during World War II, and as a veteran he was entitled to receive a parcel. When he opened the one given to him, he discovered that it had been prepared and packed by our dear friends in Shreveport, Jim and Rosie Wood. Such a coincidence was incredible—one parcel out of eight thousand sent from different cities and states in the U.S. In the parcel was a letter and a picture of these people who had become so dear to us during our first visit to Shreveport. Both Jim and my father had served in marine aviation. Jim had served in Alaska, and my father had flown to Alaska several times. Some time after our first visit to Shreveport, Jim came to Ekaterinburg as a member of the delegation to discuss with the Russian government the sending of humanitarian aid to the citizens of our city. Did he ever expect when he was buying food for some unknown Russian friend after his return home that he was packing it for his friend Paul?

Just as Jim and Rosie, and Cal and Gaye Cranor helped my parents—and therefore all our family—in hard times, so they went on helping me, especially when I went through times of spiritual collapse. Whenever I came to Shreveport on my trips to the U.S. to represent and speak about Russian Methodism, I stayed or visited with them. They became my spiritual parents, and God used them, I think, to heal me, even though I couldn't share with them all my disappointments and heartache. But they seemed to sense everything about me without my telling them. Rosie and Gaye became my second mums—sensitive and tactful, tender and solicitous. I was lucky: one mother took care of me in Russia, the others took care of me in America.

Rosie's patience was astonishing. As soon as I appeared in their house, she contrived to isolate me from all the world. She created peace and solitude, trying to teach me how to find time for myself. That lesson was something absolutely new for me. Another friend, Brenda Haley, said to me one day, "Lydia, if you don't learn to take care of yourself, you won't be able to take care of others for long, either." But I didn't take this lesson to heart right away. I really thought I should have enough strength to care for all the world.

"You can't burn the candle at both ends." When Rosie quoted this saying to me, I didn't realize she was talking about me. But Rosie didn't take into consideration my optimism and great capacity for work. Reading my soul as she alone could do, she saw other things: exhaustion and doubt. Often we would stay up long after midnight talking—about faith, my grandfather, our lives and problems. No one can listen like Rosie and Jim! And how much I received listening to them!

I worked on my first sermon in English in their house. While they entertained my children with boating and sightseeing, I went over my sermon theme again and again, trying to get my English in order. My Russian was so much richer, and I never liked to use any notes, preferring to see the eyes of those I addressed.

There were a lot of strange, even mysterious, coincidences during my stays with the Woods. We began to notice that every time I came for a visit, Rosie's air conditioner broke down, and we'd laugh about it. But the time that I was working on my English sermon, the refrigerator, the microwave, and the VCR broke as well, and the car wouldn't start! After I preached at Broadmoor, Rosie told me that a journalist, David Westerfield, asked her, "How do you feel living under the same roof with Lydia?" She paused significantly.

"What did you answer?" I asked impatiently.

"Of course I told him about all these strange coincidences," she said, her eyes twinkling. "And now everyone will be afraid to invite you for a visit." We both laughed.

Whenever I returned from a trip to the United States I felt stronger, because so many people prayed for me. But after I got back into the routine in Ekaterinburg, I would soon begin to be suffocated again by all the problems. I felt tired and worn out, as if all my strength had been pumped out of me. I was concerned, too, about the new churches that were started in other places with our assistance. They were going through hard times, just as we had. Their pastors didn't get any salaries, even though they risked everything for the sake of their churches: their families, their health, their very lives.

The Conflict over Salaries

Perhaps I was wrong to begin to fight for pastors to receive salaries, particularly since I used to say that the church is no place for fighting. But when I became a member of the committee for developing Methodism in Russia and one of the directors of the Board of Global Ministries for The United Methodist Church, I felt responsible for developing young churches. At the time, my salary was $25 a month, sent to me by the Louisiana Conference. But when I learned that I was the only pastor of our Russian churches to be getting a salary, I decided to refuse it until all the other pastors were paid. At the same time, I tried to help other pastors by sharing money I received from speaking in various churches—Ivan Kozlov in Sevastopol, Nelly Mamonova in Pskov, and my sister in St. Petersburg. I don't really know whether this action of mine played the decisive role, but in September 1993, all the pastors were put on salary. I received $500 in cash, with a note saying this was my pay for the next five months—we had all gotten a raise.

When I called Ludmila Garbuzova in Moscow to congratulate her on getting her first salary, she became very upset. She hadn't received anything. (I found out later that Bishop Minor had forgotten about her salary.) *Well, then,* I decided, *I'll wait too,* and I returned my money in sympathy with Ludmila, thinking that the sooner Ludmila got her money the sooner I'd get mine. As a matter of fact, it took six months for the mistake to be corrected and our salaries to be reinstated. I am so grateful to my family for their support during that time. The children never complained. Sergei lost his job during those months and was unable to find another. We lived on the cheapest food—potatoes and macaroni—when that was the time when there was plenty of good food in the stores, like juices, fruits, meat, cheese. Julia and Paul needed vitamins, which I couldn't afford to buy.

The decision that seemed to me such a natural one began to have, for some reason, an international echo. Rumors and conjectures began swarming around my name: "If Lydia refused a hundred dollars a month, evidently she has more money than she needs. What normal person would refuse a salary?" Others, wanting to make me comply, pressed me to take the money, so that all the talk would stop. But I'm obstinate! The more it hurt, the more obstinate I became.

Once, when I was flying with a delegation of Americans from Moscow to Ekaterinburg, one of the pastors began to take me to task. "Lydia," he proposed, "why not make us your sister church? Our church has got a lot of money. What can Broadmoor do for you?"

I was so disgusted that I wanted to snub him firmly by saying "Lydia is not for sale!" But I pulled myself together and began to tell him what was so important for our parishioners and for me about our special relationship with Broadmoor. Nothing could be as good as that. I could read in the pastor's eyes his reaction: *That's just lyricism—just nice words.* This man always held his head high, as if he were looking for something above other people's heads. His attitude proclaimed that he had come to teach ignorant Russians, and he always talked—and sang—loudly. He began a lengthy discussion with an Orthodox priest who came to our church to hear him speak, and it was clear he felt he had utterly defeated him.

After three days in Ekaterinburg, seeing what he wanted to see, this pastor felt he knew my church well enough to write a report on the church—how it was organized in the wrong way, how inexperienced the pastor was and without theological training. At the end of his report he wrote, "In a parishioner's words, this is not a church but a family enterprise." (I knew where he'd gotten that comment.)

After the pastor left I had one question: Why did he come? To criticize or to help? To breed strife or to do something kind? To reconcile us with the Orthodox church or to make enemies of us? Guests of his type created more problems for us by making my adversaries bolder in their antagonism.

The Conflict over the Prison Ministry

In September 1992, I was invited to speak to a pastors' school in Mississippi. When I told the pastors from more than two hundred churches about our church and our parishioners, many of them wept.

I was very tired when I got back to Ekaterinburg, just in time for Sunday services. During the service an announcement was made that a large group of members was leaving the church. It was a heavy blow coming to me after I had not slept for three nights in a row. *Why hadn't they told me before?* I wondered. Why hadn't they discussed everything at the church council? (Two months later, however, almost all of those who had left came back, but very quietly. They came to services, taking seats in the hall and not saying anything.) But it was not a happy ending.

Later my right-hand staff person told me, "We're all 'SOVKI.' We've all been brought up by the Soviet system. We didn't discuss anything beforehand because we were afraid. We were afraid that if we criticized anything, we'd never be able to go abroad again." With the announcement in the service, the cleavage was sharply defined, showing that everything had been thought out and prepared ahead, so that when we were told about it at the last minute, we were confronted with a *fait accompli*. I could only try to put a good face on an awkward situation by announcing at the council meeting that two of our parishioners had left the church. The two women assured all of us that working in the prison had become their vocation and they wanted to devote their lives to it.

As a result of this second split, a second Methodist church eventually appeared in Ekaterinburg, organized in February 1994—the Return United Methodist Church. That in itself was good. The more churches the better. The problem was the way it was created. Those who left us took with them the prison program we had begun with such difficulty. Actually, there were plenty of prisons to go around, and there was room for more than one program in that particular prison. And I was not the only one who went to the prison. Other members from our church were taking part. I preached only once a month, but three other members went every Wednesday. Their ministry became important not only for the prisoners but also for themselves. Yet one Wednesday the guard would not let them in to meet the prisoners, and on Sunday I wasn't able to enter the prison. Our admission passes had been taken away. The officers who used to welcome us with smiles now looked aside, embarrassed. I had to go to one of the former parishioners, I was told, to get my permit back. With that word, everything became clear. This woman's husband was on the prison board (the same man who had almost been arrested after the airlift of humanitarian aid). So now we had no access to the prison—how similar it was to the old Soviet times!

Soon after that, I asked the two women who had left our church to come to my office so we could discuss why they had wanted to leave. "I need a chair of my own, a title," one told me. "I'm sick and tired of playing second fiddle." Her words reminded me of one of our previous meetings in 1993, when she was disturbed and very upset, she said, because there was no understanding between us.

"Why don't you become a pastor yourself?" I asked, wanting to believe her.

"I haven't got charisma," she said with a sigh.

That might be true, I thought, but I encouraged her anyway. "You can become a good pastor." I wanted so much to help her, hoping that becoming a pastor would change her, help her stop smoking, and help her stop being so demanding. Perhaps then she'd find what she needed. Two months later I asked Bishop Rudiger Minor to consecrate her as a pastor along with three other Russian women and two men—Ludmila Garbuzova, Olga Kotsuba, and Nelly Mamonova—as well as Ivan Kozlov and Leonid Pirogovsky. So in October 1993 she did become a pastor.

Not long after, an Orthodox woman who knew her came to me. "Lydia," she said reproachfully, "there's no worse sin than consecrating a wrong person. You recommended someone who is far from God. You have committed an awful sin."

In the aftermath of the split there were various reactions, and no one was indifferent. Some said, "Things must not be so good in Lydia's church." My reaction was more complicated. I was disturbed, not so much by the fact of their leaving—I felt much easier without them in the church—as by the way they had left; treacherously, behind my back. That really hurt.

Healing

I went home after the service the Sunday I learned some of the members were leaving, and slumped down in my armchair. I really died that day. My body stayed in the armchair but my soul wasn't there. I felt as though it was the end—there was no time left to turn to God. I had no strength to pray, not even any thoughts. How long I stayed like that I don't know. A day? A few hours? I seemed to lack the energy even to breathe.

Then images began to form in my mind. . . .

A church in Oklahoma . . . Shawn Powell, a girl in a wheelchair, coming to me after my sermon and kneeling in front of me, kissing the edge of my skirt. I saw myself rushing down to help her get back into her wheelchair, crying, "Who am I? How can you kneel before me?"

In my armchair, I felt tears slowly rolling down my face, reviving me.

A church in Florida . . . The pastor and I were kneeling to pray in front of the altar before the service. Light streamed from the altar and a hand appeared out of the light and touched my head.

An old school in a small village near Ekaterinburg . . . More than a hundred old women had come to the service. Their church had long been destroyed and they had invited us to serve Communion. After my sermon the old women were crying, wiping their eyes with their kerchiefs. During Holy Communion, they kissed my hand. *O Lord! Who am I that these old Russian women who survived the war should kiss my hand?*" I couldn't help kissing the wrinkled hand of the next old woman.

How many blessings I had been given! How generous the Lord had been to me! And He kept on being generous. He raised me from the dead when I really had already been killed.

I opened my eyes. Strange—I'm alive!

I was still recovering when I went to visit a church in Moscow. The pastor and I met as two suffering, weeping women, who remained women in spite of everything. We were not made of stone after all! We could afford to be weak sometimes and to cry our fill.

I was frightened, though, for the other pastor. She was so pale and weak, and seemed ready to collapse. I finally wormed the truth out of her—she had been menstruating for two months and had no money for treatment. Her daughter, who was studying at the university, couldn't boast of being strong either. The food they could afford was even worse than ours. Compared to their problems, mine didn't seem so serious. And I really had a nice church and such good parishioners on the whole.

The pastor, however, had even more troubles. It was as if she had opened a Pandora's box. She had no place for services and no money to rent a hall. Every Sunday mother and daughter loaded themselves with heavy bags and went to the library, where they were allowed to hold services only because this pastor gave free music lessons to children there.

Looking at this pastor during her sermon, I felt like crying again. *My God! What is she doing to herself?* From a detached point of view, sacrificing oneself is so beautiful. But somebody has to think of those who sacrifice themselves for others, someone has to support and defend them—and not just in heaven, but here on earth. The church members couldn't do it—they needed a lot of help and expected their pastor to be strong. So she couldn't complain. And being proud and wanting to do everything well, she kept smiling, talking, and singing splendidly, infecting all the people around her with her optimism. But inside she was thinking about death.

When I tried to talk her into risking an operation, she told me, "I won't survive another surgery. I won't wake up." She had nearly died after a previous surgery. The daughter was very concerned for her mother, but couldn't help her.

In the next day or so, it became clear to me that our Lord tests the strong ones longer than the weak ones. But when the end seems to be near, He stretches out His hand and sends honest and decent people to the rescue.

I had come to Moscow because representatives of the General Board of Global Ministries were coming to this pastor's church—General Secretary Randolph Nugent, Associate General Secretary Kenneth Lutgen, and Bishop Woodrow Hearn. They had been invited for negotiations with the Russian government. I knew and trusted these people, and was always amazed at how openhearted and modest they were. So I didn't hesitate to tell them about my friend's potential tragedy. What happened then was a miracle.

It took just one day to solve all the problems—arrange the date of the operation, obtain her visa, buy her tickets. Fantastic! My friend and fellow pastor had no time to realize what was happening or to raise any objections. The very next day she was on the plane to Houston, Texas, where Bishop Hearn's family looked after her. When I phoned her in Houston, she was weeping for joy.

"Lydochka, you can't imagine what wonderful people they are! They've become my family. We understand each other without words. They've spent sleepless nights taking care of me after the operation."

This was how she was rescued, how her life and my faith were saved.

God really works in miraculous ways. In the midst of my suffering from all the stress and conflict in my life and the church, I was elected to represent Russian Methodism in the General Board of Global Ministries, and in April 1993 I went to Indianapolis for the Global Gathering—a celebration of faith and unity in the name of God—along with representatives from all over the world.

At registration, each person received a different color name tag. My tag came with a small flag and the word

Director. I didn't know what that meant, so I didn't pay any attention to it. But my friends who had come to the gathering from different churches read the tag with great surprise. "Are you really a director?" they kept asking. Some were shocked. I still had no real idea of what it meant, and I didn't have time to think about it because I had to concentrate on my speech. In front of several thousand Methodists from all over the world, I shared my story and told why Methodism was so important for us Russians. Afterwards people came up to greet me and give me their love, to say that they would pray for me and that I should be strong and not give up. In this atmosphere of love, I felt myself grow strong and happy again. I felt myself being healed.

I had been asked to take part in some workshops about Methodism in Russia along with Bishop Rudiger Minor, formerly the bishop of East Germany but now the bishop of Russia. During the first workshop, I told of starting the Methodist church in Russia. At the second workshop, when the bishop picked up on what I had said and introduced me as "an electrochemical engineer without theological education," I was hurt. But after the workshop several people I didn't know came up to me responding to this negative comment: "Lydia, don't worry. We have a proverb in America: 'If it ain't broke, don't fix it!'" Even now, two years later, I'm still very grateful to these people for their affirmation and support.

After the Global Gathering's celebration, the General Board started its work. That's when I discovered what the word *Director* on my tag meant. I came to the Board of Global Ministries as a director for Russia and the C.I.S., and was welcomed by the directors from the other countries. Then it was my turn to be surprised and shocked, to find out how much was involved in being a director and what a privilege it was for me, a beginner, to be on the board.

Each day we worked hard. But we also had time for worship services and prayer meetings. I found a prayer partner, and I also felt strong spiritual support from the board. The understanding I received and the strong concern I felt from the board members for Russian Methodism moved me deeply. *I need to be even stronger and braver than before,* was my reaction. *I must bring this good news to all Russian Methodists. God helped us to create a real church and other Methodists have a great interest in us. They all are praying for us.*

Through meeting so many wonderful, kind people—my new friends, brothers and sisters—and in this atmosphere of love, concern, and prayer, my healing continued.

Then I entered seminary at St. Paul School of Theology in Kansas City, Missouri. As I studied, I began to see all my problems in a different light and could take a detached view of them. As I studied the history of the Methodist Church and its theology, I realized with relief that all the conflicts in our church and around me were quite natural. Finally I understood that the church is just people—people with all their good points and all their flaws. That was how Methodism had developed in other countries, so one can't expect anything different in Russia, which herself is being torn into pieces. There are so many problems, one right after the other. We don't have time to forget one before others beset us. It's a pity no one told us that this is the way of the world. It's a pity Russians have thought for so long that we are to blame for everything—we're different from other nations and everything is wrong with us.

One day I was sitting on a bench near the seminary, when I stopped reading and looked around me. The fresh air, the peace, the cleanliness filled me with elation. Scores of squirrels were fussing at my feet. I looked up and saw only white clouds in the sky. Somehow that amazed me—it seemed to me our Lord was telling me that the light always wins. Then I got to thinking about my church and everything I had lived through. And when I looked up again, I saw that the sky was now overcast with black clouds. *Is evil really stronger than good?* I asked myself. *Is the dark stronger than the light after all?* But God seemed to prompt my next thought: *White clouds are above the black ones; they are higher than the black clouds.*

That truth came to me just when I needed it. It said to me that I must not try to prove anything, but I should accumulate patience. I needed to rise *above* the black clouds. There is space there. There is fresh air. There is *light*.

It was with this Light that I returned home. I had only been away from the church for two months, but I was quite a different person. I was happy and joyful, and my sermons became positive again. I could see justice and love in the world, and I thanked God for all the trials He had sent to test me. I thanked Him for my family, for our church members, and for all the friends He had sent to keep me from breaking down. And I thanked Him for all the gifts I'd received from Him.

In these last five years, the Lord has given me back my former self—the fearless, trusting, ready-to-smile dreamer. Now I can enjoy the course of events around me. I have learned not to weep because of filth and corruption and hatred. I have learned to rise high above the black clouds and see only the deep blue of the sky. When we rise up into the sky, we rush through the black clouds at great speed; then we find ourselves in such a limitless blue that everything petty and base is so unessential we forget it.

That's where my strength and joy come from. That's why I know that after strife and resentment, after misunderstanding and hatred, the realization of something much bigger and more permanent will suddenly come to me. And everyone will be able to feel it.

Learning to live at high altitude is not simple. Sometimes there doesn't seem to be enough air, and we don't have enough strength to keep our bodies going. But it's the only way for the human race, the way shown to us by our Lord. If we want to be with God, we must follow this way. A difficult way, but such a natural one, when we choose Him.